MY SUMMER OF CRICKET

MY SUMMER OF CRICKET

NIKHIL KULKARNI

Three tests, one fan and decades of stories

HEMBURY
—BOOKS—

Praise for *My Summer of Cricket*

"Cricket is an art, not a science. The beauty of cricket can be digested properly if we slow down and take the time to look, listen and immerse yourself into the experience. My Summer of Cricket takes you right into the heart of the game – allowing you to feel the energy of the players and the crowd."

Simon Taufel

Former ICC Elite Umpire, Five-Time ICC Umpire Of The Year

"There are so many cricket books that talk about the history, biographies and detail and analysis of series and/or tours. That is why Nikhil's book is so refreshing. My Summer of Cricket goes deeper into how the game of cricket has shaped Nikhil into the man he is today. I have always believed that cricket is more than a game and teaches you some wonderful life lessons. If you have ever wanted to understand why cricket means so much more to others, this book gives you a real insight."

Lisa Sthalekar

Former Australian women's cricket captain, World Cup winner and ICC Hall of Fame inductee

"For all the analysis and story-telling that accompanies an international cricket summer, there's something very pure about a fan account that embellishes both the narrative and the way we reminisce about it, and Nikhil hits it out of the park with this book."

Bharat Sundaresan

Award-winning writer and commentator

Author of The Dhoni Touch, Believe (with Suresh Raina) and The Miracle Makers (on India's 2020-21 Gabba triumph)

"Cricket is odd. Here is a team sport that's intensely personal in how it measures milestones, and how its fans experience and remember it. Few people remember it with the passion and personality that Nikhil does. This is an intensely personal love letter to the game, weaving through time, place and people. Like all good love letters, it's warm, funny and written from the heart."

Sidin Vadukut

Bestselling author, columnist, and commentator

Former editor at Mint Lounge and columnist at ESPNcricinfo

"Having been part of the game as a player and a coach across both Australia and India, I've seen how cricket is more than just sport – it's culture, emotion and identity rolled into one. This book brings that to life with warmth and insight. Nikhil captures the fan's perspective with honesty, humour and heart, showing how cricket connects

generations, communities and countries. A wonderful reminder of why we love the game."

Ashely Noffke

Former Australian international cricketer

Respected coach with a global footprint across the men's and women's game

---

"From the energy of the stands to the quiet moments of reflection, Nikhil captures what cricket truly means to its fans. It's full of nostalgia, insight and the thrill of what's to come. Love for the game and passion for nurturing the next generation shines through."

Arjun Dev

Renowned coach and mentor

Royal Challengers Bengaluru (WPL); ex-Rajasthan Royals (IPL)

"My Summer of Cricket is a joyous celebration of cricket's power to build community. Through his personal story, Nikhil reminds us that the true impact of the game lies not only in the thrill of bat and ball, the accumulation of statistics and who wins or loses, but in the friendships formed and the spirit of giving back that cricket inspires. It's a timely reminder of the joy that comes from sharing the game and belonging to something bigger than ourselves."

Geoff Verco

Charity Development Manager, The Primary Club of Australia (The Cricketers' Charity)

"My Summer of Cricket is a moving reflection on what makes the game so special. Nikhil reminds us that cricket's magic isn't just in the contests on the field, but in the way it binds families, bridges cultures and passes from one generation to the next. It's a story of belonging and connection that every cricket lover will recognise."

Professor Philip Morgan

Founder - Daughters & Dads Cricket

Co-Director of the University of Newcastle's Centre for Active Living and Learning, Australia

"Nikhil's memoir is a celebration of cricket as a bridge across cultures, generations and geographies. It captures the spirit of fandom, the joy of shared identity and his deep passion for championing women and girls in cricket. A tribute to belonging, inclusion and the power of sport, this is something that resonates with my own work through my Not for Profit Multicultural Women in Sport and my role as Multicultural Champion for Cricket Australia."

Molina Asthana

Founder, Multicultural Women in Sport, National Chair – Sport, Art and Culture, Australia India Business Council

Multicultural Ambassador, Cricket Australia

"Cricket has always been more than a game. It is memory, belonging and the quiet rhythm of life itself. In My Summer of Cricket, Nikhil reminds us that the real magic stretches from centuries to the collapses, and in the moments between, a chant in the stands, a smile from a stranger, the silence when the rain falls on an empty field. As Cricket Australia's Multicultural Ambassador, I often see how this sport carries people across borders, languages and generations. This book captures that truth with simplicity and heart. Mind you, it is not a match report, or a memoir, but it is a gentle meditation on what it means to follow something you love with devotion, to lose yourself in it, and to discover that in giving yourself to the game, the game gives something back. For anyone who has ever lived through their own summer of cricket, this will read like both a memory and a prayer."

Gitesh Agarwal

Multicultural Ambassador, Cricket Australia

About the author

A lifelong cricket tragic, Nikhil Kulkarni's first book, *My Summer of Cricket*, is an impassioned memoir chronicling the Test cricket matches between Australia and India over the 2024–25 summer. It's also a heartfelt homage to the lasting connections between cricket fans across the globe.

With a distinguished career as a product management leader across several startups and high-growth companies in India and Australia, Nikhil currently leads teams in the AI space at Atlassian. He regularly speaks on AI and product management and mentors young talent.

Nikhil is a community leader and advocate for deeper Australia–India ties. He serves on the management committee of the NSW chapter of the Australia–India Business Council and was recognised as a 2024 finalist at the Asian Australian Leadership Awards in the Corporate Category. In 2025, he was named one of 21 national leaders in Asian Australian Voices, an initiative bringing diverse perspectives into policymaking and national discourse on Australia's engagement with Asia.

A strong believer in paying it forward, Nikhil was a founding volunteer and part-time Fellow at iSPIRIT, a think tank in India aimed at fostering entrepreneurship in the software product ecosystem. He has led several programs and key events for the Indian startup community.

Nikhil's deep love for cricket is matched only by his enthusiasm for wordplay and puns. An avid quizzer, he has appeared twice on SBS's Mastermind. He is deeply invested in supporting girls' cricket and lives in Sydney with his wife and two daughters – both of whom he's trying to convince to pick up the bat!

Copyright © Nikhil Kulkarni 2025
First published by Hembury Books in 2025
hemburybooks.com.au
info@hemburybooks.com

Author website: nikhilnk.com
Author email: hello@nikhilnk.com

ISBN 9781923517219 (paperback)
ISBN 9781923517202 (ebook)

The moral right of the author has been asserted.
All rights reserved. No portion of this book may be reproduced in any form without permission from the author and publisher, except as permitted by Australian copyright law.

 A catalogue record for this book is available from the National Library of Australia

Dedication

To the most special three *ti*'s in my life – my daughters,
Neeti and Keerti, for the joy they bring every moment,
and my wife Deepti for the wonderful partnership we share.

To my parents, Indira and Narasinharao – for all
their support and blessings.

To every single cricket fan – there may be
billions of us, but each one carries their own
unique memories and experiences.

Contents

PROLOGUE 15

INTRODUCTION 17

THE RUN-UP 21

GABBA TEST, BRISBANE 35

BOXING DAY TEST, MELBOURNE 97

NEW YEAR'S TEST/PINK TEST, SYDNEY 143

THE GAME CONTINUES 161

POSTSCRIPT 179

ACKNOWLEDGEMENTS 182

PROLOGUE

Here's a bet. Ha, what a start! A book on cricket starting with a bet.

Anyway, here's a bet. Find me an Indian kid from the 80s and 90s – we're called millennials, I think – who didn't, at some point, follow cricket like it was a second religion. Go on, I'll wait.

To be honest, we didn't really have a choice. Cricket wasn't just a game. It was background noise, family bonding, national pride and personal identity all rolled into one. It taught us how to wait, how to hope, how to scream at a television set as if the players could hear us.

It's not for no reason that people call cricket a religion in India. Like me, most people from the country hold a strong association with cricket, mainly due to the number of significant memories surrounding the game. From our World Cup win in 1983 to watching the game on colour television for the first time, my generation – the hopeless cricket fans generation – has seen quite a bit of change.

Now, if we have all gone through something similar, you might ask, Nikhil, what are you trying to tell me with this book? Fair question, so let me answer it. First, this book won't be a long-winded biography of cricketing memories or a walk down memory lane, though I will be indulging in that a bit. I'll let you know what it's all about in a short while, but for now, rest assured that you'll soon be free from my introspective monologues about the past.

Second, I genuinely believe that I have my own set of special memories and situations that deserve to be shared, especially over the course of the few months that this book will cover. So, I'm writing this book as a short and fun recollection of those moments, held together by the thread of experiences I've had over the course of one summer.

But, and this is a promise, it will not be a simple narration of events. It is an attempt to showcase the deeper and intricate themes that play out in a cricket fan(atic)'s life, and talk about the beauty of them. Think of it as a summer diary. One that starts with me sneaking off to watch cricket while my family flies to India. And then accidentally stumbling into something bigger.

You won't find dressing room gossip or deep statistical analyses here, but you will find memories, madness and moments that show cricket is so much more than what happens on the field. Through the entire journey, I'm sure the inner fan in you will relate to my experiences and musings about the game.

So, what are you waiting for? Pad up!

INTRODUCTION

The thirty-year (p)itch

Have you ever followed something passionately? If you have, you'll understand that at some point, that interest becomes a part of you. Such a deep part of the workings of your mind that you don't have to consciously make an effort to think about it anymore. It simply exists as a piece of you. For me, that passion (or should I call it an obsession?) is cricket.

My earliest memories of cricket go back to the 1992 World Cup, the one held in Australia and New Zealand. Mornings in Ilkal, the small town in North Karnataka in India, where I spent my early years, were quite hectic. We still used firewood to heat water, so the whole house smelled like burnt timber. My mum would be getting me ready for school, and my dad would be rushing to leave for work. Somewhere in the middle of all that, in the corner of the house, there was a little metal radio quietly doing its job by giving us cricket updates and commentary.

That radio was where I first heard Narottam Puri. The way he described the play, the polish in his commentary, the ease with which he moved between calm and excitement stuck with me. Narottam Puri was to Indian cricket commentary what Richie Benaud was to the global game. (Maybe not in fame, but definitely in feel.)

I was probably around eight, but something about those updates cut through the chaos. For the first few times I heard him, I couldn't even make out what silly point or cover drive meant. But I kept listening anyway. And somewhere along the way, a fan was born.

Eventually, what started off as a bit of childhood curiosity turned into something else. A habit. A routine. A small pocket of joy in otherwise ordinary days. And before I knew it, the radio wasn't enough. Watching India on TV wasn't enough either. I wanted more. I started following local matches. Ranji scores. State selections. The under-19 scene. I'd scan the sports pages before anything else, zoom in on player names nobody else in the house cared about, and make mental notes like some self-declared selector. I wasn't watching the game anymore; I was tracking it. I knew which Karnataka batsman was on the rise. I had opinions on who deserved to play for India A. I wasn't getting paid for this, obviously. But in my head, I was part of the system.

And when some of those names I'd been tracking through domestic scorecards and selection snubs finally broke into the Indian team, it felt personal. Like someone from your school had made it big.

Cheteshwar Pujara was one of those guys for me. I'd been following him from his Ranji days, and always believed he would do well. For me, he was that calm, unshowy, solid-as-a-rock player you really had to watch to appreciate. I remember thinking even back in 2008 that he was ready. Just give him a chance.

> **Nikhil Kulkarni** ✓
> @nikhilnk
>
> My only wish for the New Year - Cheteshwar Pujara gets into the Indian Test Team.
>
> 8:09 PM · Dec 30, 2008

I've been a fan of Cheteshwar Pujara from long before he made his international debut.

So when he finally debuted in 2010, batting alongside the Master Blaster Sachin Tendulkar himself, scoring a fantastic 72 in a winning cause, it hit me in a way I didn't expect. Maybe some were surprised, but for me, it felt like quiet validation. Like watching a bet you'd placed years ago finally pay off. I knew he'd deliver.

I've never really kept track of how much of my life cricket has taken up. But if I had to guess, it's probably more than any reasonable person would admit. And yet, I wouldn't take any of it back. Because somewhere between the early morning scorecards and late-night replays, the big games and even the half-watched ones, the fan in me just kept showing up, again and again.

So, before we dive into the summer of 2024/25 with its Brisbane heat, Melbourne drama and Sydney chaos, I want to show you something first.

As a kid, I had a scrapbook. Not the glossy, Pinterest kind. This was an old-school notebook with pages that had seen better days, filled with yellowing newspaper clippings I'd painstakingly cut out with classroom scissors. Every time Sachin scored a century or Anil Kumble took a five-for, I'd find the morning paper before anyone else, snip out the headline, and paste it in. Some pages were crooked, some had glue stains, but it didn't matter – this was *my* record of the game. My own little archive of greatness. I guess, in a way, this book is a grown-up version of that same instinct. A chance to collect memories, freeze moments and make sure I don't forget how it all felt.

So, before we head to the stadium, I'm opening the scrapbook one more time. This time though, I'll show it to you with words, not pictures.

CHAPTER 1

THE RUN-UP

Sachin – A billion hopes

The most striking – pun absolutely intended – thing about Sachin Tendulkar, aka the Master Blaster, aka Paaji, isn't his career or his fame. It's how relatable he is.

Tendlya is the popular nickname for Sachin Tendulkar, and my very relatable association with him starts right there. I'm from the northern part of Karnataka state in India, which borders Maharashtra, the state Sachin belongs to. In that part of the world, we add *ya* to the end of your name or surname and that becomes your nickname. For example, My name's Nikhil, but everyone from my school knows me as Nikya. I've been called that name more times than I can count. So, of course, Tendulkar had to be Tendlya.

Ask anyone who grew up in India in the 90s, especially the kids, and you'll hear the same thing. We didn't want to be him just because he was famous. We wanted to be him because we believed we could be him. What made him truly great wasn't just the records or the centuries. It was how he made every kid with a bat in their hand believe that they had a shot.

That if they loved the game and tried hard enough, they could be the next Sachin. He made greatness feel familiar and somehow within reach.

Sachin's story just felt real. He was a middle-class Mumbaikar, a family man and someone who carried deep respect for the people who shaped him, especially his coach, Ramakant Achrekar. There was a quiet dignity in how he carried himself, and it made you want to root for him not just as a cricketer, but as a person. He made you believe that where you came from didn't matter as much as where you were willing to go.

And as a sportsperson? Of course, he was a legend. Not just for what he could do with a bat, but because of what the rest of the Indian team was like back then. We had a few other bright spots, sure, but mostly it felt like the whole show depended on Sachin. I've lost count of how many times the TV in our house was turned off the moment he got out, as if with a quiet agreement that if he was gone, the match was already over. My family wasn't the only one. That was the mood across the country.

For all we cared, he didn't just play for India. He *was* India.

But he wasn't just the team's identity. He built something for himself too. There are so many brilliant players whose careers faded into the background – wrong time, wrong team, wrong system. And there was a point when I genuinely worried that Sachin might go the same way. He was doing everything right on the field, but we weren't winning much. But no. He made smart choices off the field too.

From sponsorships to endorsements, he grabbed opportunities that made sense not just for him, but for India. That's a big reason he stayed relevant. He knew how to be a cricketer and a symbol at the same time. I still remember finding out about the deal he signed with Mark Mascarenhas, reportedly worth 100 Crore Indian Rupees (about US$21 million at that time in 2001). I think I just sat there blinking at the TV screen. A hundred crores? For one cricketer? It didn't even feel real. It was like someone had added an extra zero by mistake. But nope, that was the number. All of a sudden, it felt like Indian cricket had stepped into a different universe. Not because of a World Cup win or some magical series, but because one guy had made himself that valuable. And somehow, it made the rest of us believe the sport was going somewhere bigger too.

And then there's something people don't talk about enough – how long he played.

Sachin started playing when Kapil Dev was still around and signed off after we won our second One Day International (ODI) World Cup. That's twenty-four years of international cricket. Just international, without even counting the Indian Premier League (IPL), the domestic grind, the charity matches, or the fact he was still playing the Masters tournament a week before I sat down to write this. The guy just keeps going.

And it wasn't just the longevity either. It was the pressure of walking out with a billion people holding their breath every time he took guard. That's not normal. That's ... I don't even know what that is.

For me, and for every kid in the 90s, Sachin wasn't just an idol. He was a journey. A steady presence. A quiet rhythm. A reason to believe in possibility. He's why I still get goosebumps when someone mentions Sharjah (the iconic stadium). He's why I still believe good things can happen if you care hard enough. Thank you, Tendlya.

The fanboy in me wouldn't rest until I showed you this, so here goes.

I was on national TV. I was in Mumbai, squeezing in time between work outside the stadium at Sachin's last Test match. If this doesn't make you nostalgic, I don't know what will. There's a bit of a story in the video, but I'll let you watch it for yourself and find out.

Nikhil at the Wankhede Stadium in Mumbai for Sachin Tendulkar's last innings

Match fixing – fanatic to fan

If I make a list of the top ten people who come to my mind when someone says cricket, the names of Sanjeev Chawla and Mukesh Gupta will figure prominently. Funnily enough, they weren't cricketers. They weren't even coaches or analysts, nor were they match administration or stadium owners. Heck, they weren't even a match director in a stadium as who decides which camera gets telecasted onto the TV every few seconds. (Sounds like a fun job until you realise you have to keep track of twenty-plus cameras at once.)

Sanjeev Chawla and Mukesh Gupta were, in fact, bookies involved in the match-fixing scandal of 2000 that shook my faith in the game. I remember reading about it in the news and my reaction, for all my experience following cricket as a fifteen-year-old, was of utter disbelief. It edged on being comical; I just couldn't believe something like that was possible, especially when the names involved were people the cricketing world held in such high regard.

One of those names was Hansie Cronje. He was a hero to me, especially as he led the South African team shortly after the apartheid ban was lifted. I looked at him with the same sense of awe that I looked at some of the legends of the game. Given how young he was when he captained the team – twenty-four years old – it was surprising to see the strength with which he innovated.

One such incident was from around the 1999 World Cup when he came onto the field wearing an earpiece to communicate with coach Bob Woolmer. There were no regulations around this at the time, but the umpires eventually asked him to take it off. Now you might say that using the earpiece wasn't in good spirit. I disagree. If you look at the history of cricket, it was innovated not through rules and regulations, but players tweaking their play style in small, seemingly insignificant ways that weren't rule-breaking but gave them a slight advantage over the opponent. Consider overarm bowling for example, which developed from the then-standard practice of underarm bowling when players slowly started raising their hands to gain speed and accuracy.

I digress. Back to the case. When the Delhi police announced they had solid proof of Cronje's involvement in booking matches with Sanjeev Chawla, I simply didn't believe it. Of course, like with any sensational news, a number of wild conspiracies were floating around. They didn't help either.

A few months later – or weeks, I can't remember – came Cronje's confession, where he said he only proposed the offer of throwing the match to his team, but no one acted on it. You can imagine the ruckus this caused in the adults who followed cricket. But, for teenage Nikhil, it was world shattering. Sport, as a follower, is something you put your heart and trust into. It's something that motivates and inspires you to be better (much like Sachin did to the entire Indian youth). It's not just what happens on the field, it's the aura of it that you carry around every day. That's what was tainted by these actions.

For a few months, at least, I lost my interest in following the game. Every ball I watched seemed to come with the question – what if this was fixed in advance? It's really exhausting to watch anything when you're not fully involved.

Eventually, I did regain the passion and interest, but this event marked a significant juncture in my journey. From then on, I wasn't a fanatic who followed every single thing about the game anymore, I was just a fan who loved the game. (Not a bad way to be, in hindsight.)

Sourav Ganguly – a fresh start

It was 2003. I was in a university called the National Institute of Technology (NIT) in Surat, the diamond city of India. (Fun fact: about 90% of the world's diamonds are polished in that city alone. I wonder how they keep the thieves out!) I didn't know much about the outside world, though. While the college wasn't a jail, the campus rules meant most of us were back in our hostels before the city even lit up. If you know Indian universities, you know on campus doesn't always mean open access. It just means that life runs on curfews, mess timings and the occasional stolen moment of freedom.

One advantage of being cut off from the outside world is that the world inside starts running on its own rhythm. You line up for meals together, race to finish laundry before lights out, and somehow end up knowing everyone's snack stash hiding spot. One of the manifestations of this community was the cricket-watching experience. For every India match, a bunch of us who probably only knew each other's names would gather in the boys' hostel, in the one room that had a television, and watch the match together.

To describe the scene in one word – colourful. By design, the university took in students from all corners of the country. So, each match was a mixture of dozens of cultures sitting together, commenting in twenty-plus languages. Amidst all those differences, we bonded as one.

One such incident was watching the 2003 World Cup, with Sourav Ganguly leading the team. Brilliant man, he was. His captaincy is one of the best things to have happened to Indian cricket. He took charge during a time when trust was at an all-time low (due to the match-fixing scandal), and he still managed to turn the team around with his strong focus on developing emerging talent. For a team recovering from scandal, you couldn't have asked for a better captain – he backed a group of youngsters to the hilt and always led from the front, literally and figuratively. The amount of self-confidence – a level that was unseen and unexpected from an Indian captain – and the belief he showed in the team was reflected in each and every young player who shone under his leadership. If Sachin was the shoulder on which India's hopes rested on, I'd like to believe that Ganguly was the one who built pillars that would take over the weight when the maestro had to go.

When I hear his name, though, I have two very distinct memories, one auditory and the other visual, which simply play out in my mind without permission. The visual memory is his memorable celebration during the 2002 NatWest Trophy final at the Lord's Cricket Ground, a moment of pride for India. I still remember the match. It was the day Yuvraj Singh and Mohammed Kaif showed the world that the coming generation is a different beast altogether. We won, and if that wasn't enough of a highlight, seeing the captain take his shirt off and celebrate like a lion that had just won its dinner seemed, for lack of a better word, glorious. I'm not sure what it was for him – it could well have been nothing but the adrenaline of the moment – but for every Indian out there, it was a reflection that we'd made it. That in just fifty-five years after independence, we were in a state to openly celebrate in the heart of the cricketing world. I remember how every Indian cricket fan walked with their chest puffed out for the next few days.

The auditory memory, probably even more memorable than the celebration for me, was Sir Geoffrey Boycott's commentary on Sourav Ganguly's batting. He used to call him the Prince of Calcutta. (Calcutta was pronounced in a way I'll never be able to explain.) He had a way of bringing out the beauty in his play that your mind wouldn't immediately perceive, and that made it very fun to listen to. If not for him, I wouldn't have enjoyed Ganguly's batting as much, nor would I have fallen in love with brutally honest commentary.

Anyway, I digress. We were all watching one of India's games during the 2003 World Cup. It was examination time, and the student council negotiated with the professors to start the exams earlier so we could be back in time for the match. (Yes, it really was that serious for us.) There were more than a hundred people from different states throughout the country, which meant that whenever something went wrong, you would hear colourful words in about a dozen different languages at the same time. Quite the experience.

For the young-adult Nikhil who was still reeling from the shock of match-fixing, those days of watching cricket together were pivotal. Each match made me realise that even though there would be a thousand things in the background that I don't like or approve of, the sport, the act of playing it, is pure – and with that purity came its ability to be loved. The proof was all around me in the form of a hundred young boys whose eyes burned with fervour, forgetting caste, creed, religion, just to root for the eleven players they call their own.

IPL – the madness that somehow made sense

For Indian fans, 2007 brought with it a disappointing one-day World Cup that was in stark contrast to the 2003 campaign where India made it to the finals. The team didn't even make it to the Super Eight, so morale in us fans was low, especially because we knew legends like Rahul Dravid, VVS Laxman and Sourav Ganguly were towards the end of their careers. In contrast, it was also known as the Year of the Great Australian Team for how well they played in the tournament. India did win the T20 World Cup later that year, so that boosted people for a bit.

Anyway, if that was the global scene for Indian cricket, the last quarter of the decade brought something else entirely into the national cricketing scene – the Indian Premier League (IPL). It should come as no surprise when I tell you I had a very strong opinion on the IPL when it was announced: confusion and chaos.

Let me explain. As we entered 2008, the IPL was all over the news. There were Bollywood stars like Shah Rukh Khan and billionaire industrialists like the Ambanis owning teams, and almost every famous personality in the nation had something to say or do about this tournament. I was also surprised at the concept of players being auctioned. While I've come to accept it now, at first glance, the concept of auctioning players seemed undignified. As if that wasn't enough, Rajeev Shukla was everywhere (still is, surprisingly), controversies dialled up, and the usual sportsman–actress relationship whispers were getting louder and louder.

A few things did excite me, though. The fact that I'd get to see players who played against each other fiercely in international cricket were now in the one team – Harbhajan Singh and Andrew Symonds being my favourite example – and how youngsters who just entered the scene would get to share the locker room with legends like Sachin. It was truly something I didn't know how to feel about. But overall, my reaction for the first year of the tournament was, *'Ye Kya Tamasha Chal Raha Hai Bhai?'* (It doesn't have the same ring to it in English, but it translates to *'Bro, what kind of circus is this?'*)

Looking back, I think the purist in me just didn't like the change, while the child in me couldn't wait for some entertainment. Over the years, the child won. For someone who never forgot the betrayal of trust that was the match-fixing scandal, the IPL taught me to just watch the game for the fun of it. Matches happened within an evening, so there was no spending nights analysing next-day strategy, or spending innings breaks breaking down everything that had happened. It was just a game and, with its low stakes, was meant to be taken lightly.

While the match part of the tournament sorted itself, I found myself highly interested in the business part of it too. You see, back then, international matches never made me realise how big of a business cricket is. But now, watching tens of thousands of people flock into stadiums every match (59 matches to be precise, for the first IPL) and hearing rumours that media rights/advertisement contracts were being bid on for absurd amounts, it was hard to ignore it.

Amidst all my internal thoughts, there was a hard truth no one could deny: the IPL was the best stepping stone Indian cricket could have asked for. I think it was marketed with the slogan Opportunity Meets Talent during one of the earlier years, which couldn't be truer. It was a platform for the entire nation to watch and judge the players. For the first time, everyone talked about who was to be selected for the national team, a pastime that until a few years before was enjoyed only by hardcore fans. And for me, who has been a passenger-scout for India all my life – daresay I'd be a very good one if I got into it professionally – watching every follower in the nation talk about it felt like a blessing.

Eighteen years later, the IPL is one of the most dominant tournaments in the cricketing world. I don't watch a lot of it anymore – timings really don't suit Australian dwellers, ha ha – but its growth, and the spot it put India in, is a matter of pride for the Indian in me.

End of the beginning

My Summer of Cricket starts with me in the heat of things, ready to get on a flight and watch my first (and the series' third) match in Brisbane. Before that, however, I think it is important to go through what happened in the year before (2024) that led to me attending those matches in the first place.

Personally, 2024 was a huge year for me in terms of cricket and community. It was the year I did the Daughters and Dads Cricket program with, you guessed it, my daughter. It was a nine-week program focused on developing the bond between fathers and daughters through the use of sport, in this case cricket, which helped us make some amazing memories and form strong bonds. I'll talk more about this program in a few chapters – I have a few plans around it, fingers crossed!

Additionally, it was also the year I was very active in the Australia–India bilateral collaboration space. It started with the Australia India Youth Dialogue (AIYD), where I was part of the 2024 Australian delegation. One of the guests was Hon Warren Kirby, my local Member of Parliament and Co-Chair of the NSW Parliamentary Friends of India. It felt genuinely heartening to see my local MP playing such a meaningful role in fostering the Australia–India relationship. At the closing ceremony, I had a quick chat with him, and he said he'd introduce me to someone named Irfan Malik. I didn't know who Irfan was at the time. The very next day, I got a call from Irfan asking if we could meet.

We caught up, and it turns out, he was working on New India House, an India-focused space at SXSW Sydney. SXSW Sydney is the Asia-Pacific edition of the iconic Austin, Texas, festival – a wonderful fusion of innovation, tech and culture. It was happening in a few weeks. He needed help. I said sure. One thing led to another, and suddenly I wasn't just helping, I was deep in it. Program management, content, branding, marketing. Everything. All pulled together in a few weeks. I had done a lot of volunteer work in India, organising events in the tech and startup space, and like muscle memory, all of those things came back.

Irfan, by the way, is one of those people who knows everyone. And somehow, he's everywhere too. If you showed interest, like I did, he brought you in. No drama; just action. He is the Australia India Business Council (AIBC) National Associate Chair and the NSW chapter President. His energy and passion for all things Australia–India is incredible, and if you're in his orbit, you see your own energy and passion increasing manifold. Irfan is a true force multiplier.

That experience ended up pulling me further into this community space that I hadn't fully tapped into before. These days, I work with him more formally as part of the NSW Management Committee, but the real story is how a chance meeting turned into a whole new chapter. Thanks to AIYD and the New India House, which was a big success, by the way, I made so many connections with people in the Australia–India bilateral space.

All this interaction with the Australian–Indian community also grew my interest in the greatest connector of the two countries – cricket.

There was no moment of realisation when I decided I wanted to watch the three Tests in person, at the stadiums. I knew for a long time that the Border–Gavaskar Trophy was happening in the summer of 2024–25 and thought it would be cool to go watch one of them. The twist, however, was that we (my wife, my kids and I) were planning to travel to India around the same dates. With the kids growing up in Australia and their grandparents in India, we've always tried to make sure they get real time together to build bonds, share stories, soak in the chaos, the food, the accents, the roots. You know, the stuff that doesn't happen over video calls, and the summer break is the only time we can make it work for long enough to actually mean something.

On the other hand, I was very keen on attending at least a few matches of this series, and my desire grew every day. It would be my last opportunity to see Virat Kohli and Rohit Sharma play a full-fledged Test series on Australian soil, and I couldn't bear the thought of missing it. So, I did what every sane husband would do and communicated this with my wife. (You thought I'd done something crazy, didn't you?)

Unsurprisingly, she was very supportive, as she has always been when it comes to my passions – whether it's quizzing, cricket, or even something as intensive as writing this book. She offered to leave for India with the kids a week earlier to match up with my schedule and asked me to join them later in the summer when my trip was finished. So, in awe of my supportive wife – seriously, she's awesome and I couldn't be more grateful – I sat down to draft an itinerary for my Summer of Cricket.

CHAPTER 2

GABBA TEST, BRISBANE

Day 1

The moment I finally said, 'Alright, I'm doing this, I'm going to Brisbane to watch the Test,' Brisbane said, 'Too late, mate.' Not in so many words, of course. But the ticketing website did flash a smug little Sold-Out banner across the screen, and that felt close enough. Turns out, while I was busy weighing the pros and cons of leaving my family a week early, thousands of other fans had already clicked Book Now.

But there was no going back now. I was fully committed.

And I wasn't ready to un-commit. I'd already crossed that invisible line in my head. So I did what felt natural: I booked my first flight. A Saturday morning departure to Brisbane, which would put me in the city right as the match was about to begin. No stadium seat, no accommodation sorted, no plan beyond just being there. But still, I was going. Somehow, the rest would sort itself out. That's the thing about Test matches. You don't just watch them. You give yourself to them.

It felt like a good decision. Until I checked the calendar.

The flight was on a Saturday morning. I had booked it on a Thursday night. Which left me exactly one day, Friday, to do everything else: packing, tying up loose ends at work and cancelling a long-planned meeting with a colleague who had flown in from overseas. We'd been meaning to catch up for months, except now we weren't. I sent him a short message the night before. Said I had to travel unexpectedly and hoped we'd catch up the next time he was visiting Sydney.

So Friday became a blur. I tossed clothes into a bag, scrambled through work emails and told myself that I'd somehow sleep on the plane. By the time the Saturday sun rolled around, I was exhausted but triumphant, standing on the kerb with my suitcase, waiting for my Mercedes-Benz V-Class Uber.

Yes, you read that right. A Merc as an Uber. I booked a normal Uber X ride from my house in North-West Sydney to the airport, but it turned out that the Uber gods really liked me that day and sent a six-figure car to pick me up (at least I think it was). I did a double take. Then a triple take. Briefly considered checking the plates to make sure I wasn't accidentally hijacking the ride meant for some touring celebrity. But nope, it was mine.

The driver looked young, maybe twenty-nine or thirty, and Indian. Naturally, I got curious. You don't expect a car like that to show up under Uber's standard ride option. So, a few minutes into the trip, I asked him about it.

He laughed and said yeah, he gets that question a lot. Turns out, he drives this Merc around mostly for premium bookings and events but occasionally switches on Uber for fun when he has free time, and doesn't really care to register for the premium rides. Said he only did it because it was a good way to meet interesting people. I told him that sending this particular vehicle to pick up someone going to a Test match might just qualify as divine intervention.

That's when the cricket chat began. He mentioned that he often gets bookings from Indian celebrities who visit Sydney. Nothing too specific, just that a lot of his clientele end up being film and cricket folk. And then, almost as a side note, he dropped it: apparently, he knew Virat Kohli from his U-19 days in Delhi. Used to call him Chiku Bhayya.

Now, almost every millennial from Delhi claims they knew Virat in one way or another. Just like every Bangalorean in the 90s – are they gen X? I get confused – knew someone who knew Javagal Srinath or Anil Kumble. It's almost a rite of passage. But there was something different about the way this guy said it without any performance or pride that made it seem real.

We spent the latter half of the ride silently as I was playing out the steps from getting off the plane and finding a seat at the stadium, but I was smiling throughout. It wasn't because of the Mercedes or even the celebrity angle, but the sheer ordinariness of the moment. I hadn't even left Sydney yet, and already cricket had found a way to slip into the story. Through a stranger, through a memory, through a name that somehow still felt personal to someone.

I didn't want to read too much into it. But as omens go, it felt like a good one.

We pulled into the airport just as the light began to shift, basking in the rays of an almost-orange sky. I stepped out, stretched, did that awkward pat-down to check for my phone–wallet–keys, and reached for my suitcase in the trunk. And that's when I saw it – the car right behind mine. Another Uber. The door pushed open and out stepped … Abhinaya. The very colleague I'd cancelled on less than twenty-four hours earlier.

For half a second, I froze. Not because I didn't want to see him, but because I genuinely felt disappointed that he might be flying back to India.

I stood there thinking, if he's leaving the country, I should've made time.

Then he looked up and spotted me. He smiled in a tired, slightly amused way that said, *Really? Here? Now?* I smiled back.

We walked toward each other. With a is-this-really-happening look on my face and the same thought in my head, I asked him where he was headed.

'Brisbane,' he said. 'To watch the match.'

My jaw didn't drop. But I think my eyebrows shot up far enough to make that point. We were on the same flight. Later, when I got to my seat and saw he wasn't seated beside me, I felt oddly reassured. If he had been, I think I would've looked around the cabin for hidden cameras. It was already starting to feel a little scripted.

We checked in, got through security and found a quiet place to settle down, swap cricket memories, and eventually had the catch-up that was supposed to happen earlier in the week.

We made our way to the gate and boarded. Different seats. Same direction. The story had already begun.

Once I got to my seat, I finally did what I'd been meaning to do for about two trips now and pulled out *The Wrong Man* by Tim Ayliffe. It had been sitting in my bag for months like an unpaid bill. One of those books I kept carrying around with the full intention of reading, and then never actually reading. I'd opened it once, maybe twice, but never properly.

I've always had a thing for thrillers, especially spy and espionage thrillers. Back in engineering college, I used to haunt the public library and burned through their collection so fast that eventually I started pestering the librarian for new arrivals. At some point, she gave up and just began setting books aside for me. I'd gone through most of the Ken Folletts, Frederick Forsyths and Robert Ludlums they had.

One stand-out from that time, I'm talking about the early 2000s here, was *Bunker 13* by Aniruddha Bahal, one of the rare espionage stories set in India. Bahal actually led the sting operation on match-fixing in Indian cricket while at *Tehelka*, the magazine known for its investigative journalism. So yeah – espionage, journalism, cricket, it all blurred together in the best way.

Even the book in my hand was a signed copy that I found in a bookstore near Avalon Beach, so I was very excited to read it. As the flight began to take off, I finally started reading the book. It's set in Sydney, which made it all the more amusing that I was reading it just as I was flying out of Sydney. One of those little ironies that only makes sense when you're half-asleep at 35,000 feet.

...

We landed in Brisbane well after sunrise. The city looked like it had been politely woken up. Tall buildings still stretching, a river curling through the middle like it didn't need to be anywhere urgently.

Right as I was about to get off the plane, I found a ticket on Tixel, an online ticket reselling marketplace and bought it instantly. Finally! I was going to the match. The ticket was only for today, but I only needed to take the Test one day at a time.

In India, I would've probably just shown up outside the stadium and asked around. Done that plenty of times. The old-school method: look lost, scan the crowd, and sooner or later a guy with tickets (and no official badge) would magically appear. I've given a fair bit of business to those unofficial vendors over the years. (Fun fact: that's how I got into the Wankhede Stadium for Sachin's last Test match as well, and we all know how that turned out for me.)

But I wasn't sure if that same approach would work in Australia. I didn't want to risk being the only one at the Gabba waving a cardboard sign that said, 'One ticket please'. So yeah, a reseller marketplace. Click, done. The match was on.

Abhinaya and I shared an Uber since our hotels were close enough to each other. He booked it, and it arrived in exactly five minutes. Not a Merc this time, though. Which was probably for the best. Any more cinematic omens and I'd start looking for a film crew. I got to the hotel well before the allotted check-in time, but the front-desk guy was kind enough to let me freshen up early. A small mercy after the past two days of scrambling.

Around 9.45 am, I stepped out again, suitcase abandoned, backpack in place, ready to head to the ground. I opened the Uber app out of habit. Then stopped.

I noticed a bus stop right beside my hotel and, more importantly, a small horde of people gathering there, all dressed like they were headed to a cricket match. Jerseys, hats, one guy was already waving a flag as if he were in the stands. It was obvious. They were going to the stadium.

So, I figured, if everyone's going, I might as well join them. I ditched the Uber plan and caught the next bus to the Gabba.

The Brisbane stadium is called the Gabba. I'd heard it called that my whole life by commentators, friends, broadcasters, but I'd never actually stopped to think why it was called that. (As a trivia buff, that's kinda shameful.)

It wasn't until I was on that bus and glanced out the window and saw a street sign that had Woolloongabba and Brisbane Cricket Ground on the same board that I figured that the word comes from the suburb the stadium is in. A whole lifetime of cricket commentary and I'd never put it together. I just assumed Gabba was a vibe, or something like that. A cricketing aura. But no, it was a suburb. A literal place. That kind of thing makes me unreasonably happy.

The bus curved off the main road and turned onto a street lined with cricket jerseys and takeaway coffee cups. The energy shifted. You could feel it before you saw anything. People sat up straighter. Phones came out. Someone near the front started humming the title song of the movie *Chak De! India*. (It's possibly the closest thing we have to a national sports anthem.)

And then, there it was. The Gabba.

Big, round, and weirdly tucked into the middle of everything. No grand entrance. No sweeping boulevard, it's just there. One moment you're passing a 7-Eleven, and the next, there's the stadium, rising out of the street like it's been dropped from the sky and no one had time to clear space for it. It wasn't imposing. It wasn't dramatic. But it was something.

And in that first moment, before the match, before the stalls, before the seat-hunting and applying a ton of sunscreen, it felt like I'd arrived at the start of something I didn't quite understand yet.

As I got off the bus, the first thing I noticed was the noise. It wasn't too loud or deafening, but it was everywhere. The low murmur of early morning excitement. Kids with painted faces. Grown men already yelling 'Indiaaaaa, India!' like it was the fifth day. Someone was selling those inflatable clapper sticks. Someone else was already asking if they had a spare ticket. It felt alive.

The path into the stadium was lined with stalls. At least half of them seemed Indian oriented, selling food, jerseys, chai, even mini tricolours you could clip onto your bag. You could buy a cold drink, a flag, a kathi roll and a Rohit Sharma fridge magnet all within ten metres of each other. The whole place felt like a cricket-themed Diwali market. I didn't pay much attention to them, given I had another fourteen days of cricket to go, but one little tent caught my attention: a *gilli-danda* stall. If you've never played *gilli-danda*, imagine cricket's rural ancestor – not really, but the visual works – stripped down to two sticks, zero protective gear and absolutely no concept of health and safety. You place a small, pointed stick (the *gilli*) on the ground, and use a longer stick (the *danda*) to flip it into the air and smack it as far as you can. No wickets, no pitch, no rules that anyone fully remembers. It's basically baseball plus cricket for kids with no equipment and a lot of spare energy.

I hadn't played it in twenty-five years. Maybe more. But muscle memory does funny things. I picked up the *danda*, got into a stance that felt half-natural, half-performed, and swung myself back into childhood.

I spent a good fifteen to twenty minutes just soaking it all in; way longer than I should've, considering play was about to start. But it struck me how much of this was built around the Indian crowd. The food, the flags, the playlists, even the Hindi stall signs. It wasn't just flavour, it was strategy. Apparently, there's a saying in the Australian cricket circles that only matches played against India or England actually turn a profit. Standing there with a *gilli-danda* in one hand and a chai in the other, I could see why.

...

I scanned in, climbed a set of stairs that felt unnecessarily steep, and stepped out into the Gabba. And there it was.

Clean lines, soft morning light, a big round bowl of a ground with the kind of quiet confidence that didn't need to shout. It wasn't trying to overwhelm you because it didn't need to. I stood still for a moment just taking it in. The sound of warm-ups, early crowd buzz, the unmistakable smell of beer and fried potatoes.

The field looked sharper. The boundary ropes looked tighter. Everything looked like it mattered more when you were inside the stadium.

I made my way to my section, dodged elbows and backpack straps, and dropped into my seat just as Usman Khawaja and Nathan McSweeney were walking out. India had won the toss and opted to bowl.

Jasprit Bumrah had the new ball. The crowd settled into that Test match hush of waiting for the match to start, and it soon did.

First delivery: a dot ball. Of course.

I shifted in my seat, took a sip of water, and casually looked to my right. And nearly choked. Sitting next to me, in full tricolour, flag in hand, as if he'd just stepped off the broadcast feed, was Sudhir. Yes, that Sudhir – Sudhir Kumar Chaudhary. The body-paint guy. The one you've seen in almost every India match, home or away, waving the flag like it's his full-time job, which honestly, it kind of is. You don't spot Sudhir. You just assume he's part of the landscape. Like the sightscreen or the third umpire. And now, apparently, a part of my row.

He was mid-phone call. Calm. Focused. Not posing or flag-waving; just sitting there. Like this was normal. I didn't say anything. What do you even say? 'Big fan of your ... aura?' I simply smiled and let both of us be.

The cricket didn't last long.

Rain showed up before lunch and never really left. I think we got through maybe 12, 13 overs? Long enough to see Bumrah get into a rhythm, short enough that you wondered if you'd imagined the whole thing. But honestly, I didn't mind. I had fourteen more days of cricket ahead. If anything, it felt like a soft launch. A teaser. Enough to say, 'Yes, I've been to the Gabba,' without having to commit to any real analysis.

If you've ever been part of a Test match crowd walking out after a rain delay, you'll know the crowd exiting the stadium is in a certain kind of mood. It's not disappointment exactly, more like quiet acceptance. A stadium full of people who took a day off, packed their lunches, travelled across town (or the country), and are now pretending they didn't really mind that it ended early. People aren't upset. Just a little off rhythm. Conversations feel slower. No one's in a rush, but everyone's leaving.

That's where everyone was. Mentally already halfway to dinner.

And then, just as I walked out of the seating area into the outer ring of the stadium, I noticed something strange.

People weren't leaving. In fact, they were lining up, just along the edges of the walls and standing with their back toward the wall.

At first I thought it was some sort of crowd-control thing. Maybe there were stewards guiding people through a specific gate. But there were no stewards. Just fans. Dozens of them, shoulder to shoulder, forming a kind of corridor between two sections. And they weren't walking through it. They were waiting.

Then one guy, who looked around my age but maybe younger, walked down the centre. Everyone started cheering. Not loud, not performative. Just goofy, spontaneous applause. A few high-fives. Someone yelled, 'Well played!' like he'd just scored a gritty fifty. The guy raised his hands and did a little exaggerated bow, laughing all the way through.

And then the next person walked through. Same thing. More cheering. Someone else danced their way down. A kid sprinted through like he was about to open the batting. And slowly it hit me: this wasn't for the players. It was for us. For the fans, by the fans.

It wasn't part of any big plan. Just something a bunch of people who seemed to agree that if the match wasn't going to give us a memory, we might as well give one to each other. A kind of unspoken, crowd-sourced send-off. Equal parts silly and sincere.

And somehow, it worked.

At first, I didn't walk through. I just stood to the side, watching it all unfold. Snapped a few pictures. Laughed quietly as strangers played along like this had always been part of the Test match experience. No one was performing. Everyone was simply enjoying it. It felt unscripted in the best possible way.

After a while, a gap opened up. Someone must've left from the far end of the tunnel. And suddenly, there was space right next to where I was standing. So I slid in without any announcement or hesitation. Just joined the line and became part of the tunnel.

This entry meant that for the next few minutes, I was one of the first faces people saw when they stepped in, and I got to see everyone's initial reaction as they had the same lightbulb moment I'd had realising what the tunnel stood for. A few looked surprised. Some grinned. One guy did a victory lap spin as he walked through. And like everyone else, I cheered, clapped and played my small part in making this ridiculous, beautiful thing keep going a little longer.

The whole event lasted maybe five more minutes after that, probably because my seat was near the front of the tunnel, meaning I was one of the last twenty-five or thirty people to exit. So I just stayed there, clapping them out, one by one, until there was no one left to clap for.

Nothing significant happened that day cricket-wise, but I walked out with a satisfied smile on my face, the one that usually shows up after a full day's play.

Somewhere on the way back to the hotel I remembered I might actually be eligible for a refund. I'd bought the ticket off a guy on a resale site, and we'd messaged a bit before the match. I texted him, informing him about the rain and the refund, and he said he'd be happy to return the money. 'Just send me your payment details,' he'd said. 'As soon as I get the refund from the organisers, I'll forward it on.'

Which, in hindsight, felt optimistic.

I sent the details. Got a polite thumbs-up emoji. And never heard from him again. No refund. No reply. Just digital silence.

Still haven't received a cent. But hey, at least he was nice about ghosting me.

...

By the time I got back to the hotel, the buzz had started to wear off.

It wasn't late, just barely past three, but the city already felt like it had moved on from the match. The lobby was quiet and the lift smelled vaguely of sunscreen and damp polyester. I peeled off my socks, checked the weather forecast for the next day (again), and opened WhatsApp to send a couple of tunnel pictures to the family group chat.

Then I remembered I hadn't really eaten anything.

The plan had been to grab something inside the stadium, but then the rain came, and then the tunnel happened, and then the guy selling samosas left, so dinner suddenly became the only event left on the day's schedule.

I headed out around seven in the evening, mostly by instinct. Didn't google anything, just walked until I found a place that didn't look too empty. Eventually I found an Asian place with warm lights, actual food and a few people who looked like they'd also just come from the Gabba. I didn't bother with the menu. I saw laksa and closed it. It's my fallback order. The one dish that almost always hits the middle of the bat. Want some comfort food to get over a rough day? Laksa. Something to celebrate? Laksa. Too hungry to think what to order? Laksa, of course.

The laksa hit the spot, like it always does. Warm, familiar, no unnecessary surprises. I ate slowly, half-scrolling through the day's rain memes, half-thinking about what tomorrow might bring.

And then, on my way out, just as I stepped onto the footpath, I spotted Morne Morkel – ex-South African bowler and current bowling coach for India.

He was just there. Wandering the street like any other tall South African looking for dinner in Brisbane. Maybe he was also hunting for laksa. Maybe not.

I smiled. He nodded. We made eye contact, and I said something as I approached him that I don't even remember. It was the kind of throwaway line you say to a cricketer because you feel like you should. He replied with something polite, gave me a selfie, and that was that. It lasted maybe thirty seconds. Still counts.

I got back to the hotel, kicked off my shoes, and checked the weather one last time. Still not great. But somehow, it didn't bother me.

Day 1 was technically a washout. Didn't feel like one though.

Day 2

Sundays always have a vibe of their own, don't you think?

You could throw me into a random day, and just by the way the morning light hits the room, my body somehow knows it's a Sunday. A day meant for big plans, or no plans at all. Maybe it's a placebo, or maybe my body's developed a highly cyclical routine over twenty years of working in IT, but Sundays never fail to put me in a good mood.

As you've probably already guessed, Day 2 of the Brisbane Test match was a Sunday. I woke up early, partly due to excitement, and partly due to the time-zone difference. Seriously, whose idea was it to have different cities on the same side of the country operating in different time zones – but here we are. In classic Sunday fashion, I decided to win the morning to win the day. Threw on some sneakers and stepped out for a walk.

Some quick googling told me the Mount Coot-tha botanic gardens weren't far from where I was staying. And since I was already out and had a 10,000-steps-a-day streak I wasn't planning to break, I figured I might as well do it surrounded by trees. Nature wins over laps around the hotel corridor any day.

And lush nature it was. I expected neatly trimmed hedges and the occasional labelled orchid. What I got felt closer to a tropical forest. The kind where you start questioning if you've accidentally wandered off the public path and into a documentary. Towering trees. Strange bird calls. Zero people for long stretches, which was either peaceful or mildly concerning, depending on the moment.

I kept walking.

No podcasts, too, which would have been weird any other time because I haven't walked without a podcast for ages. But amidst those trees, it felt right. Just me, my steps and the slow Brisbane morning unfolding under a heavy sky. Eventually, I found myself near the Wheel of Brisbane, that big Ferris wheel near South Bank, and an artificial beach I didn't know existed. I sat there for a bit. Let my legs cool off. Watched a kid try to build a sandcastle with what looked like a takeaway container.

Normally I'd have snapped a quick photo. Maybe send it to the family group or post it with a caption that only made sense to me. But this time, I switched to video. Flipped the camera, framed my face with the beach behind me, and recorded a quick morning message for my daughter.

It was still night back home in India, so I told her it was morning here and showed her the sand and the giant wheel slowly turning in the background. Said something about how the whole family should come visit someday. I didn't think much of it at the time, but looking back, that little video was the start of a quiet ritual that would follow me across cities and stadiums, tucked into the margins of the game.

I got back to the hotel, changed and left again without wasting time. Still had that early-Sunday momentum going. I took the bus again, same stop as yesterday, minus the *gilli-danda* break.

Turns out, getting to the Gabba is fairly straightforward from where I was staying, it's just it seemed a lot more complicated the day before because of the crowd and me constantly checking my phone to see if my ticket was real. I reached the stadium in under ten minutes, which made me question everything about the logistics of Day 1. Honestly, I'd spent more time yesterday just thinking about how to get there.

Because I was early, I landed up near the front of the queue. And there's something mildly entertaining about being part of the first batch of people standing outside a stadium gate, staring at the still-shut gates like they might open faster if we collectively willed them to. It gave me faint Mumbai-local-train flashbacks. Except here, no one was pushing. No fake limp to get ahead. No one pretending they didn't see the line. This was the civilised version. Cricket, but with footpaths.

Once the gates opened, everything moved quickly. Security checks, bag scan, the usual friendly interrogation about whether my water bottle had any other liquids. And then I was back inside.

The light felt different today. Brighter. It was the kind of crisp, cloudless morning that makes you feel like the game will definitely go the full day. No weather report refreshing required.

I made my way to my bay, found my row, and took my seat. It was a good one. High enough to see field placements, low enough to hear the thud of a proper shot. So I sat down and thanked the guy sitting next to me. He was the one I'd bought the day's ticket from on Tixel. (His wife couldn't make it, apparently.) I gave him a quick thanks and he nodded like we'd just completed a small business transaction, which we had.

As players started trickling onto the field for warm-ups, I spotted Virat Kohli deep in conversation with Ravi Shastri near the boundary. They weren't whispering. They weren't laughing. Just standing close to the rope, looking like whatever they were discussing mattered more than anything else. Could've been team balance. Could've been golf handicaps. Could've been whether the Gabba needed a roof. No way to tell.

The conversation went on for a few minutes, then Virat jogged off and started kicking a soccer ball around with Bumrah like nothing had happened. Classic Test match vibe: intense one second, completely casual the next.

...

By the time play resumed, the sun was out and the Gabba crowd had warmed up properly. Khawaja and McSweeney walked out to continue the innings. Bumrah had the ball. And for the first hour or so, things felt manageable. Khawaja didn't last long, getting caught behind off Bumrah.

McSweeney was still trying to settle in. It took him around 40 balls to hit his first boundary; a neat-enough shot, but not the kind you remember. He scratched around for 9 runs off 48 deliveries before nicking off. Not much, but he'd done just enough to get through the morning slowly.

And then came the real problem for India: Travis Head.

He walked onto the field like he owned it, and he did. After just a few odd balls of settling in, I don't think there was an over where he didn't hit solid shots to the rope. The amusing part was that Smith, at the other end, was doing it too. Usually in Tests, one guy attacks while the other holds. It's a seesaw. But this? This was a full-blown, double-sided headache. Every over had a boundary. One from Head, one from Smith. It was relentless.

While Travis was clearly the heavy hitter between the two, it wasn't him that kept my eyes on the pitch. It was Smith. Head was the chaos, Smith was the rhythm. Every time he left a ball, twitched, nudged one behind square, I found myself smiling. He wasn't dominating. He was *settling*. And that's what made it better, because I've seen this version of Steve Smith before. The one who doesn't look dangerous until you realise he's on 78 and isn't even in form.

I have a theory. There's a special category of batters who seem to level up the moment they play against India. Doesn't matter how they've been playing, who's bowling, or what city the match is in, they just *wake up*. Marvan Atapattu, Shivnarine Chanderpaul and Mohammad Yousuf are all members of that slightly cursed club. For a while, Steve Smith was the chairman. And while the last few years had dulled that edge a bit, watching his century felt like a throwback. The hands were soft. The footwork was tight. The brain was doing whatever Steve Smith's brain does. He was back.

Head got to 150 like it was nothing, and by then most Indian fans were more interested in the forecast than the scorecard. Like, 'How much longer do we need to sit through this before the universe steps in?'

Luckily, the universe did show up – in the shape of Jasprit Bumrah with a semi-irritated expression and a plan. Late in the day, he just switched gears. The pace went up, the lines got tighter and the Australians, who'd spent most of the afternoon batting like it was a net session, suddenly started playing him like he was bowling grenades.

By stumps, they were 405 for 7. Still dominant, but the smugness had dialled down a touch. Enough to help Indian fans sit a little straighter on the bus ride home.

I did too – sit a little straighter on the ride back. Not because I was rooting for either team specifically. But because I'd just watched two world-class batters take something ordinary and quietly turn it into a treat for the fans. That's the thing about Test cricket. When it's doing its job well, you don't always notice it in the moment. But by the end of the day, everything has shifted from the scoreboard to your mood and the way your shoulders sit.

I didn't go straight back to the hotel. Ended up wandering the same street as the night before, this time choosing a different spot. Partly out of curiosity, but mostly because their sign said laksa in a font large enough to count as a personal invitation.

That day had been a lot. And sometimes, you just need your comfort food.

Day 3

The next day, I woke up feeling it.

Not emotionally, but physically. Two days at the ground, and my back, neck and right shoulder had filed a joint protest. Turns out, plastic seats and Queensland sun aren't the kindest combination when you're no longer twenty.

However I was feeling, two days in the stadium taught me one thing – preparation is key. A half-sleeved tee and a burger with chips for meals were fine for one day, but when you're planning to watch the entire match, that doesn't suffice. So I rested a bit more, wore a full-sleeved shirt, shortened my morning walk to a quick Coles trip to stack up on food, and headed to the stadium bright and early; with a ticket in hand that I brought off the official website. In fact, I was one of the first people at the gate. This meant I got to hear all the sweet, sweet language that got thrown around when people get mad that there's a line to enter the stadium and the gate doesn't open before the stated time just because they happened to be early.

The gates opened and I walked in just around 9.30 am, feeling weirdly proud of myself. Shirt? Sorted. Snacks? Stocked. I'd finally figured out how to do this properly.

Found my seat, looked around and nearly laughed. The Indian dugout was right there. Not touching distance, but close enough that I could've thrown someone a samosa if they looked hungry. There was a bay in between, maybe six seats wide, apparently reserved for people the players invited to the match. But from where I was, I had a full view. Coaches, support staff, the actual team benches. All there. Not behind glass. Not hidden away in some air-conditioned bunker. Just a few rows away.

Most of it was empty at first because the boys were still fielding. But I kept glancing over anyway. You never know when something happens. A quiet word. A stare. One of those half-laughs between overs. For once, I didn't have to imagine it from a camera angle. I could see it.

The last three Aussie wickets were supposed to fall quickly. That was the plan. But apparently no one told Alex Carey. He walked in and immediately started swinging like he had an early lunch booking, so their innings went on for quite a bit longer. He added about 70 runs before someone finally got him out. Four hundred and forty-five. That was the final number. Not massive, but definitely enough to cause some internal bargaining.

India was finally up. A few people around me gave that half-nod you see when a meal arrives at a restaurant. Like this was long overdue. I sat up straighter, waiting for the cricket about to come and wishing that the clouds appearing in the sky wouldn't decide to pour water over my dreams.

But 17 overs later, I think the entire fanbase of India collectively willed the rain to show up. Let me explain.

India's innings started with a bang, quite literally. On the first ball, Yashasvi Jaiswal cracked a clean boundary through cover. The crowd roared.

Next ball: he was gone.

And from there, it was like someone had knocked over the first domino. Everyone just followed the opener. Edges, misjudged leaves, bad shots, good bowling – take your pick. The scoreboard was stuck but the wickets column was moving along just fine.

By the tenth over, the clouds started to darken. I remember looking around and seeing heads down, phones out and a couple of people already trying to guess how long until the rain hit. And this wasn't some sudden collapse either; it was more procedural. Like the team was politely excusing itself, one wicket at a time.

Seventeen overs in, four wickets gone, and the batting looked about as sturdy as a paper plate in the rain. So yeah, when those clouds started to make it drizzle, it was a relief.

The play paused, but I hoped the rain would start soon. The drizzle started, then stopped, then started again. That annoying kind of rain that doesn't commit but just hangs around to mess with you.

I checked the forecast a few times. Nothing helpful. The radar looked like abstract art. So I just stayed put, unwrapped the lunch I'd picked up from Coles that morning and let the afternoon drift by. There wasn't much else to do. The stadium never officially emptied until half an hour later when they announced the day's play was called off.

The stadium felt very weird, then. Two rain call-offs in three days and we hadn't gotten through the first innings yet. To symbolise my feelings toward the weather – and because I desperately needed at least one photo of me in the stadium – I got my neighbour to click a photo of me shrugging at the sky and sent it to a few of my friends who were following the game from India. And it stuck. Every time the weather played games over the next few matches, I'd send them a new shrug photo. Slightly different background. Same expression. By the end of the series, I'd created a weather report in meme format.

On the bus ride back, I struck up a chat with an older gentleman who'd also been at the match. He was a local – a Brisbanite? A Brisburbian, is that what they're called? I'm still not sure. He looked clearly unimpressed.

'Rained again?' he asked, already knowing the answer. I smiled.

He shook his head and muttered, 'Dunno why they schedule matches here this time of year. It always rains.'

It wasn't said with anger. More like the weather had let him down before, and he just didn't expect much from it anymore. I nodded along, partly agreeing, partly wondering if I'd just booked myself into the soggiest five days of cricket all summer.

Day 4

The next morning started the same way the last three had – with fond memories of laksa from the night before and light rain in the forecast.

I wasn't even pretending to be optimistic anymore, though the sky looked bright, as if it was asking me to keep up hope. Still, I packed my Coles stash, threw on my thick shirt again, and headed out early.

I got to the Gabba a little after the gates opened, and the play had already started. By Day 4, only the die-hard Test match fans were still around, so I had the luxury of buying the ticket at the stadium and perusing the ticketing options for a seat of choice. So I picked the same seat as yesterday. Not for superstition, just for continuity. I knew the view, knew where the dugout sat, and knew the prospect of catching discussions between team members was too good to give up on.

By the time I got to my seat, one wicket had already fallen. Of course it had. And for a while there, it looked like we were setting ourselves up for a good old-fashioned follow-on.

For the uninitiated, a follow-on is Test cricket's version of being told to run another lap at school because you came last – you're exhausted, already trailing, and instead of a break you're sent right back in. In practice, it means that if your team bats second and still ends up trailing by 200 runs or more, the other captain can just say, 'Nah mate, we're good. You lot go again.' And that's exactly what it looked like we were heading toward. Something India had avoided since 2011.

So, when Rohit Sharma – whose wicket fell as I entered the stadium – walked out and Ravindra Jadeja stepped in, avoiding the follow-on wasn't some minor checkpoint. We still needed 170-odd runs just to dodge it. Which, with the way things had been going, felt like asking a cardboard boat to cross the Brisbane River.

But then, something shifted. Slowly.

Jadeja walked in, bat tucked under his arm, and paired up with Rahul, who had already decided he was going to stay at the crease until someone physically removed the stumps. It wasn't a partnership that lit up the scoreboard, but more like stubborn resistance. Two blokes drawing a line in the dirt and saying, 'No more'. Every run was hard-earned. Every leave was deliberate. And every over survived was a tiny sigh of relief in the stands.

But then, just as the partnership was starting to feel like it might actually do the job, it broke. First one, then the other. And just like that, we were left needing 33 runs to avoid the follow-on with the tail of the batting order exposed and time in the day still ticking.

And then came Akash Deep and Bumrah. Not all heroes wear capes. Some wear pads, gloves and helmets. They didn't strut, they didn't swing wildly. They just did what tailenders are supposed to do, and then some. A few risky shots here, a few textbook blocks there, and slowly, stubbornly, they dragged us past that dreaded follow-on mark. They'd saved the day for India.

It wasn't glamorous, but mate, it was effective. By the time the scoreboard clicked past the follow-on mark, the applause in the stands was that of gratefulness. Even the coaching staff were celebrating like they'd just won the match.

A few overs later, the umpires had a quiet word, pointed at the sky, and called stumps. Bad light, apparently. No one argued. We'd avoided the follow-on. That was more than enough.

Just as I was stretching my legs and processing what had happened, I spotted a familiar figure doing a slow, deliberate walk around the boundary rope – not on the field, but just outside it, where the journalists and ground staff usually hover. Even from a distance, the bright shirt, shoulder-length curls and easy saunter gave him away. It was Bharat Sundaresan.

Now, I know this book isn't meant to be a who's who of cricket media, but if you care about the game even a little, especially its stories, its characters, its messiness, you should know about Bharat. He's one of the most distinctive cricket journalists out there, not just for his wardrobe or his voice, but for how much sheer love he brings to the job. He's the guy who once spent six years (six years!) tracking down Patrick Patterson, the West Indies fast bowler who terrified batters in the late 80s and then seemingly vanished. Bharat went looking for him because he wanted to know what happened. Because cricket deserves to remember its ghosts, not just its gods.

That article, when it came out, hit me harder than most fiction ever has. It wasn't just a profile. It was an excavation. The work of someone who believed that no story is too far, no effort too much, if it helps understand this maddening, beautiful game a little better. And for me, reading that piece was one of the few times I felt like someone out there got it – the same unreasonable, heart-first way I chase cricket across cities and time zones and ticket queues. No, I'm not comparing us. Not even close. But I saw in Bharat's obsession a mirror of my own, just angled differently.

So, when I saw him circling the Gabba in his colourful shirt and notebook in hand, I didn't hesitate. I called out, 'Bharat!' He turned, surprised for a second, then smiled and walked over. We chatted for maybe a minute – nothing too deep, but enough for me to tell him how much I'd followed his work, especially that six-year chase for Patrick Patterson. I think I even called it one of the greatest pieces of cricket writing I'd ever read. He laughed, thanked me, and happily posed for a selfie before moving on. It was quick, casual, unplanned, but it meant a lot. Seeing someone who'd gone to such obsessive, beautiful lengths to tell a cricket story reminded me that being a fan is a full-time job. And that sometimes, the people who tell the stories are just as much a part of the game as those who play it.

As the crowd began to thin out, I stayed back a bit longer. Not to beat traffic or wait for rain, but just to linger. The game had actually gone on without interruption. The sun had held out. And for once, Brisbane hadn't felt like a raincloud with a stadium underneath.

There were no Indian players around, of course, but Jake Fraser-McGurk (Australian international T20 and ODI batter) was in the bay next to mine, quietly taking it all in like the rest of us. I snagged a quick photo with him. Then, as I was about to head out, umpire Richard Illingworth wandered near the boundary rope, and I somehow managed to get a snap with him too.

What a day! No fanfare, no big gestures. Just a good day's cricket, a few surprise cameos, and a soft Brisbane evening drizzle to end it all.

I didn't head straight to the hotel. Instead, I wandered back to the same street I'd eaten at two nights earlier and let my feet decide dinner.

Another bowl of laksa because, of course. Fourth one in four days. At this point, it was less of a craving and more of a tradition.

Not much else needed to happen after that. Just a quiet walk back, a bit of stretching to make up for the stadium seats, and a vague sense that the match, and this trip, were slowly clicking into place.

Day 5

By Day 5, no one was really expecting a result. The weather forecast still looked dicey, there were 21 wickets left to go, the match was limping toward a draw, and even the most committed fans were starting to glance at their flight times more than the scoreboard. But I bought a ticket at the gate and showed up anyway. Because that's what you do. You block out five days in your calendar, you show up for all five. Simple.

The sky looked like it hadn't slept. Thick clouds hung low and broody. Even the Gabba felt quieter than usual. You could tell people were here more out of stubbornness than belief. The kind of crowd that shows up because they said they would, not because they thought something magical might happen.

And I was one of them, walking in with my usual supplies, nodding at the same steward, slipping into the same bay, trying to will myself into hoping for a result.

India's last wicket fell not long after I sat down. And just like that, the question of the morning shifted: what would Australia do now?

Roughly 80 overs left in the day. A lead of 175. Too little to declare straight away because on a pitch like this, any team with decent intent could chase that in a day. So they had to bat. But not for long.

If I were them – and yes, I gave it some thought – I'd bat for 20 overs, score about 100 runs, take the lead past 275 then unleash the bowlers and go hunting for 10 wickets with 50 to 60 overs left. Enough time to win. Enough lead to draw. It's these kinds of delicate questions that Test cricket lives for. Every over matters. Every run has a purpose. And with the series locked at 1–1, this wasn't just another day of cricket – it was a five-day chess match with five fielders around the bat.

That's what I think their plan was too. Bat 20 overs, pile on a hundred and send India back in with 50 to survive. But the match didn't start that way.

India's bowling looked oddly polite. Not defensive, exactly, but no one was really attacking too. And Australia's openers weren't connecting either. Not with intent, not with timing. It's like both teams were waiting for the other to blink first.

And it was Australia who blinked first. Three overs in and wickets started to fall like dominoes. What should have been an easy 100–2 was now looking like it would result in an all-out.

Suddenly Australia started swinging. Desperately. More wickets fell. India took seven of them, which I didn't see coming. Travis Head and a couple of others managed to find the boundary here and there, and their total edged into the 80s. Even then, nothing really clicked. But the Aussies got what they needed and pushed the lead to 275 before declaring.

It was still anybody's game. But now it was Australia's to win.

The equation was simple: India had 275 runs to chase and 56 overs to bat if the weather cooperated. Not impossible if they treated it like an ODI, but after four days of play, an ODI level of energy is tough. Even the sky knew it – the clouds that had been hovering all morning hung back a bit longer, just to see how this might end.

India came out to bat after lunch, but honestly, it barely counted as an innings. They faced all of two overs before the skies made up their mind. Play stopped at 2.33 pm. The restart was scheduled for 2.54 pm.

That never happened.

Instead, we got drizzle. Then a bit more. Then the kind of persistent, annoying rain that doesn't look dramatic but refuses to leave. Slowly, Day 5 began to slip quietly into irrelevance.

By 3 pm, most people had stopped pretending. A few die-hards stuck around under umbrellas, but the rest of us knew what this was now: a waiting room with no appointment.

At around half past three, the match was officially called off. Drawn. Done. No fireworks. No handshakes in the middle. Just a slow trickle of people walking out, quietly absorbing the fact that after all that effort – the flights, the food queues, the sunburn, the rain delays, it ended exactly where it had started. All square.

Still, I didn't regret a thing. Sometimes, showing up is enough. (And I also had another ten days of cricket to go.)

...

I stuck around for the post-match ceremony. Not because I was expecting anything grand – we'd barely played enough cricket to fill a highlights reel – but because I figured I'd come this far and might as well see it through. Plus, something about watching players receive their little medals and say things like, 'We'll take the positives,' always feels like a comforting ritual.

That's when the news broke. Quietly at first. Someone a few rows behind me said it. Then someone in front looked up from their phone and repeated it with a little more certainty. Ravichandran Ashwin had announced his retirement.

I didn't react right away. It felt like one of those things you wait to hear from a real source before you believe it. But the murmurs kept spreading, and eventually the news confirmed it. That was it.

In that moment, a lot of things from the last three days started making sense. All that odd tension around the Indian dugout – the constant buzz, the pacing, the unusually animated conversations. I'd noticed it, sure. I'd even wondered what was going on. But since this was the first time I'd been seated so close to the team, I just assumed that was normal. Maybe they were always this intense?

Now, though, in hindsight, it all looked different.

Maybe that's what Kohli and Shastri were talking about so intensely on the boundary line on Day 2. Maybe that's why Ashwin, despite not being in the playing XI, had spent so much time deep in discussion with staff. I'll never know for sure, and I don't need to. But it felt like I'd brushed past something significant. A quiet little piece of cricket history, unfolding just metres from me.

I stayed in my seat for a while after that. Not out of shock or sadness. Ashwin had earned his moment, and I wasn't close enough to him as a fan to feel anything personal. But more because I wanted to let the moment breathe. Cricket gives you these strange pockets of stillness sometimes. You can't chase them. You just have to sit still long enough and let them arrive.

Eventually, I got up, walked out of the Gabba for the last time, and made my way back to the hotel. The suitcase was half-packed already, filled mostly with merch and dirty laundry, so it didn't take long. But before calling it a day, I headed out one last time for dinner. And yes, it had to be laksa. Not because I hadn't tried other options (I did), or because I'd found the best bowl I'd ever had (I didn't), but because sometimes you want to end something exactly the way you started it. Five days. Five bowls. No regrets.

Back in the room, I zipped up the suitcase, double-checked my charger situation and caught a late-evening ride to the airport. No Mercedes this time, just a regular Uber.

The flight back to Sydney was short – barely enough time to take a nap, but long enough for my mind to start replaying everything. Not just the cricket, though. The weirdly nice feeling of waking up early every day excited for the game. The strangers I'd shared buses, rain delays and crowd reactions with. The taste of Brisbane laksa. The human tunnel. The surprise retirement. And that one morning message I'd recorded for my daughter that quietly kickstarted something I didn't know would continue.

It hadn't been a perfect Test. Far from it. But something about the whole trip, from the commitment and the silliness to the slow burn of five days at the Gabba, had left a mark. There was plenty more play to go, but this was the start. And somehow, even a soggy, interrupted, half-baked Brisbane Test felt like exactly the right way to begin.

Interlude

It was after five straight days of cricket, laksa and plastic stadium seats that my back finally gave up. Not during the game. Not while walking to the stadium. Not even while standing for an entire human tunnel. No, my back chose Sydney Airport's baggage carousel 4 to stage its little protest.

One wrong bend to yank my suitcase off the belt and boom, something clicked. Or popped. Or maybe just sulked. At first, I did what any self-respecting man would do: pretend nothing happened. I stretched a little, walked it off, told myself it would go away. It didn't. By bedtime, it was less twinge and more existential threat. Sitting hurt. Standing hurt. Sneezing was practically a crime.

It was mildly poetic, really. Five days at the Gabba watching other people push their bodies to the limit, and it was my own suitcase that brought me down. Not the best welcome home, but it did set the tone for what was to come …

So, by all accounts, I probably *shouldn't* have hiked the Grand Canyon Track in the Blue Mountains a day later. My back was still stiff from the airport suitcase incident, and any sane person would've used the break between matches to recover, especially with more travel and stadium time coming up.

But after watching players grind it out for five straight days, I wasn't about to let a little back pain take my wicket. I've got two kids now, and as they grow up, I'd love to take them camping, maybe even on one of those wild week-long treks where you sleep under the stars and carry everything on your back. But, if I'm going to do that someday, I need to make sure that part of me doesn't disappear today.

So, when I saw a clear weather window the following morning, I made the call: "Tomorrow, I will hike the Grand Canyon Track, bad back be damned."

Plus, it was a loop. Which, in my mind, meant safety. You start at one end, walk a few hours, end up right back where you began. How bad could it be? I told myself I'd take it easy. Start early, go slow, pack protein bars, carry a raincoat, and be responsible. To be fair, I did all those things. I left home at 4.30 am in the dark, drove through a fog thick enough to warrant a searchlight, and reached the Blue Mountains just as the first light filtered through the trees. At that moment, any lingering hesitation disappeared.

Adventure had overridden common sense. Again.

By the time I started the walk, I'd completely forgotten I even had a back. The sprain disappeared somewhere between the trailhead and the first misty overhang. Maybe it was the cool, damp forest air. Maybe it was the anticipation. Or maybe it's just that when you're alone in the middle of a canyon, with towering cliffs on either side and the crunch of gravel underfoot, your body doesn't get to complain. You're in it. You keep walking.

I've done a few long walks before: Spit to Manly, Coogee to Bondi, a bunch in the northwest of Sydney, but this one had a different kind of stillness. The kind that makes you forget all the worries of your world and just exist as simply as the trees and the rocks. It makes you realise how loud your life usually is. Somewhere along the track, I also passed a waterfall so tucked into the rock it felt like a secret valley.

The whole loop took maybe three hours, give or take, but I didn't check the time once. When I finally emerged back where I'd started, soaked, muddy and buzzing, it felt less like I'd completed something and more like I'd remembered that I could still do this. That I could do anything I wanted to.

Of course, the quiet bliss didn't last. Within five minutes of finishing the loop and sitting back in the car, I could feel a deep, slow ache radiating up from my lower back like it had been patiently waiting for me to stop playing adventurer. By the time I backed out of the parking spot, I was wincing at every turn.

I drove straight to what I can only describe as our family's hunting ground: the main street in Katoomba (also called Katoomba Street). It's the one with all the cafes, bakeries and bookstores. Exactly the kind of organised chaos that makes it the perfect launchpad for any Blue Mountains outing. For us, it's tradition. We stop there before *anything*. Fuel up, figure out what the day holds – bushwalk, scenic railway, whatever, and then return in the evening for a second round of eating before heading home. So naturally, that's where I went.

I wasn't particularly hungry (protein bars can do that to you), so I decided I'd earned a massage instead. Long walk, lingering back pain, no rush to get back home – why not? I picked a place at random, limped in, managed to get myself onto the table. Honestly, it wasn't bad. Peaceful music, warm towel, minimal small talk. Things were going surprisingly well.

Until they weren't.

The moment I got up from the massage table, my spine started jiggling. Not in a cute, loosened-up, yoga-retreat kind of way. More like a faulty suspension bridge that had just lost its last bolt. I smiled politely, nodded my thanks, and shuffled out with the grace of a wounded flamingo with stiff limbs, trembling core and a mind in full panic.

By the time I reached the parking lot, my back had officially given up.

Whatever structure was holding it together had melted. It felt like jelly – the tragic kind that wobbles when you breathe. I slid into the driver's seat in slow motion, limbs folding like wet cardboard, and just sat there, stunned. Breathing shallowly. Hands on thighs and a spine negotiating every micro-adjustment like it was drafting a ceasefire agreement.

I think I stayed like that for thirty minutes. Could've been longer. I considered calling a friend. At one point, I even considered calling an ambulance. I considered staying there forever and letting nature reclaim the car. Eventually, I shuffled to a pharmacy, grabbed a bottle of water, a heat patch and some pain-killers, and returned to my vehicle-home and took what can only be described as a car nap for the injured and spiritually defeated.

Memo to future self: if your back is already broken, don't get a massage that tries to liberate the bones. You will not walk away better. You may not walk away at all.

...

With a couple of days left before Melbourne and not much else on the calendar (aside from an eye test, which, let's be honest, doesn't make for gripping storytelling), I figured I'd shift gears. No more national parks. No more heroic massages. This next stretch was going to be about food. My back was still tender, but my appetite had clocked back in for duty.

I've always liked Sydney's outer suburbs. Not just for the food, but for how they feel lived-in, unpretentious and blissfully indifferent to trends. As long as you're hungry, you're welcome. Once you cross a certain point on Parramatta Road, there's this half-joking term people use called crossing the latte line. On one side of the line are designer dogs, $7 cold brews and people who use words like umami unironically when describing avocado toast. And on the other side: families, real spices and restaurants where the signage might be peeling but the food doesn't miss.

It's not a perfect split, obviously, but the contrast is hard to ignore. I like both Sydneys. I've lived in both Sydneys. But when I want a proper meal – not an experience, just good food – I usually head west.

Christmas Eve felt like a good time to explore. It was twenty hours after the trek, my back was semi-functional again, and my taste buds had started dropping hints. So I started asking around. First up was my regular taxi driver, Sayed. He's Afghani and always up for a chat, so I figured he'd have a recommendation. He did. Without missing a beat, he said, 'My home'.

Which was sweet, but also wildly unhelpful.

So I asked my colleague at work, also Afghani, and also generous with food advice. Her answer? Same thing: 'My home'.

At this point I began to suspect that no Afghani restaurant in Sydney had ever passed quality control within the Afghani community. It's either home cooking or bust. And, honestly, I was tempted. I would've happily eaten on the floor, shared stories, maybe helped with the washing up. But I also didn't want to show up with a Tupperware container and hopeful eyes. So, I pushed for a plan B. A restaurant I could walk into without knowing anyone's grandma.

They both gave me the same answer: Merrylands. Not a specific place in Merrylands. Just Merrylands. Like the whole suburb was one giant open-air recommendation. 'Go there,' they said. 'You'll find it.' And weirdly, I trusted that.

I suppose it's the same way I react when someone tells me they're craving Indian food. I never rattle off a restaurant name. I just say Harris

Park and leave them to figure it out. There's a kind of quiet magic in these immigrant subcommunities – if you're meant to find something good, you will.

So, off to Merrylands I went.

I didn't have a restaurant name but I had Google Maps, a free morning and a vague sense that grilled chicken was involved. I searched for Afghani kebabs and filtered for the usual signs – 100-plus reviews, at least four stars, preferably some blurry photos of grilled things. That's how I landed at Kebab Al Hojat.

It was everything I wanted it to be. Tucked into a no-frills strip of shops, sun-washed signage and zero pretence. The smell of charcoal hit me before the door did. Behind the counter, a man in a welding helmet calmly tended to skewers, face inches from the heat, as if negotiating with the fire itself. That grill looked like it had opinions, and he wasn't taking any of them.

I ordered grilled chicken and naan and the plate came out heavy and steaming with that kind of spice-mottled char that tells you everything's going to be okay. I ate like someone who'd earned it. Which, frankly, I had – physically, emotionally, spiritually.

Afterwards, I did what I always do after a good meal in a new suburb. I wandered. Around the block, past Kabul House, Kabul Barber, Kabul Travel. It felt like a local universe operating on its own rhythm, with or without visitors like me.

On the way back to the car, an ice cream place called Kabul House Sheer Yakh caught my eye (I later found out that 'Sheer Yakh' literally means 'Milk Cream'). And God, if that wasn't the best ice cream I've ever tasted, I genuinely don't know what is. Just three scoops of something cold, thick and impossibly creamy; like the very essence of milk had been churned, whispered to and frozen into silk. It didn't melt; it unfolded.

With every bite, I could feel my childhood back in India – every kulfi I'd ever chased down the street, every glass of *badam* milk I ever slurped on a hot afternoon – rushing back.

This isn't a sponsored book. But if I don't tell you to find that place and try that ice cream, I'm doing you a disservice. So, if you happen to be in Sydney, go. Immediately. Go.

...

The next day, Christmas morning, was still. Most places were shut, as expected, but I wasn't quite ready to surrender to toast at home. I had a day left before flying to Melbourne and the idea of a warm breakfast in a quiet suburb sounded like a better plan than anything festive. I opened Google Maps half expecting nothing and found a Sri Lankan place in Pendle Hill still showing Open Now in bold green. That was enough.

I drove over, expecting it to be a glitch, but sure enough the lights were on and the aroma hit me before I reached the door. I ordered a dosa and two vadas. No frills, no queue, no conversations about holiday specials.

I sat inside, no plans, just good food and time to spare. Just me, a metal plate and the low buzz of a kitchen still doing its job. The food was simple, spiced just enough to remind me I was alive. And that someone, somewhere, had decided that feeding strangers on Christmas morning was a public service. That breakfast, complete with its crisp edges, soft centre, the right amount of chutney, felt like a small kind of blessing.

The next day, I'd be on a flight to Melbourne for a whole new adventure. But for that one slow morning, dosa and vada felt like a perfectly reasonable way to ring in Christmas.

The Gabba, it turns out, isn't just a vibe – it's Woolloongabba, the suburb.
A lifetime of cricket commentary and I'd never put it together.

A gilli-danda stall outside the Gabba – two sticks, no rules, pure childhood.
Hadn't played it in twenty-five years, but one swing and I was back.

With Sudhir Kumar Chaudhary at the Gabba – India's most recognisable superfan, draped in tricolour and devotion.

On a rained-out day at the Gabba – when the cricket didn't give us a memory, we fans built one ourselves: the tunnel.

The weatherman meme – live rain updates for friends in India trying to decide between sleep and cricket.

With Bharat Sundaresan at the Gabba – one of cricket's finest storytellers, and one of this book's earliest believers.

In Merrylands, Sydney – at Kebab Al Hojat, where Afghani grilled chicken meets fire, spice, and a chef in a welding helmet. Unpretentious, unforgettable.

On the Grand Canyon Track in the Blue Mountains near Sydney – bad back be damned, the mist, the cliffs and a tucked-away waterfall made me forget everything else.

With Nick Hockley, then CEO of Cricket Australia – at the Boxing Day Gala at NGV, sharing my wonderful fan experience and swapping stories about the Dads and Daughters program.

Catching up with Drew Ambrose, AIYD mate and investigative journalist – in Melbourne – good food, great stories, and even better company.

At the MCG cloakroom – I handed over a blazer and they brought out a hanger. A hanger! At a cricket ground. I was amazed, and a little bit in love.

The beer snake in Bay 13 at the MCG – slithering through the crowd like a living creature, built cup by cup, cheer by cheer. Messy, yes, but more ritual than nuisance, a celebration with its own unspoken code.

With Aman Gaur at the MCG during the Boxing Day Test – fellow AIYD alumnus, thoughtful conversations, and a shared love for the game.

From dusty schoolyards back in India to the bright lights of John Cain Arena – kabaddi in Melbourne felt both familiar and completely new, a spectacle somewhere between AFL and wrestling.

On the Yarra in Melbourne – an Indian group played 'Yaara O Yaara', and it hit me: in Hindi yaar means mate, Australia's favourite word.

With Boria Majumdar at the MCG – a familiar face from cricket books and broadcasts, and just as passionate in person as he is on screen.

By the Yarra at the Royal Botanic Gardens, Melbourne – a painting, a pause, and a scene that always takes me back to that lovely afternoon.

At the MCG – 100,000 seats empty just days after I'd seen it packed, yet it still felt full. A temple of cricket where even the silence carries a roar.

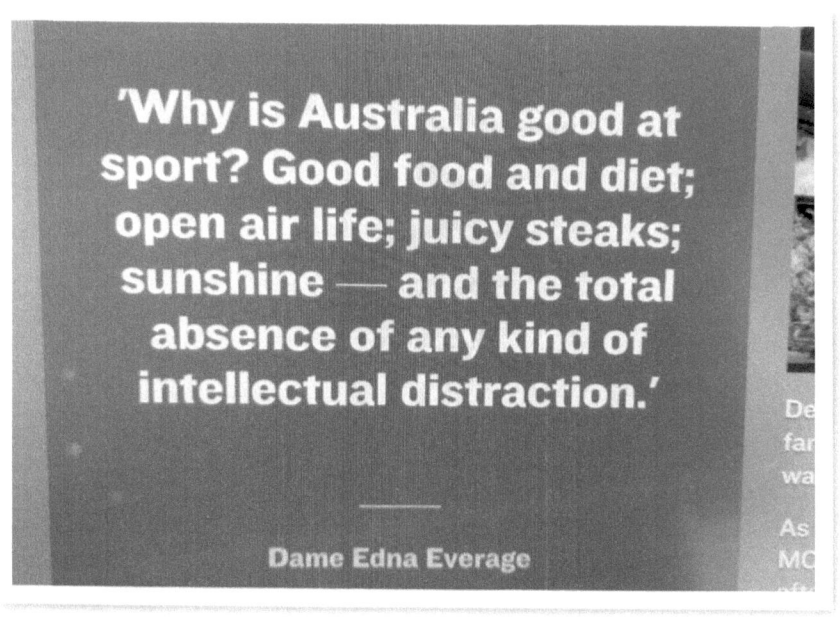

Well, what can I say to this? Sunshine, steak, and zero intellectual distraction – the recipe for sporting success, spotted at the Australian Sports Museum at the MCG.

Breakfast with the Primary Club of Australia at the SCG – tradition, conversation, and cricket with a cause, where every duck supports athletes with disabilities.

Making a quick point to Harsha Bhogle on the sidelines of the Pink Test in Sydney – at a fundraiser for girls' education, blazer still on, me fading fast, him somehow full of energy at 10 pm.

The SCG in all its glory for the Pink Test – Sydney always shows up, and it's even brighter and louder when India is in town.

Nearly a million voices stitched into one unforgettable summer, with new records at every ground. Grateful I was there to feel it.

At a 24/7 study library in Dharwad, my hometown in India – our workdays ran on Australia hours, surrounded by students chasing futures bigger than themselves, with ambition hanging in the air like incense.

At NICE Academy in Bangalore – my daughter in the nets with Inchara and Shreya, two young cricketers chasing the game with quiet grit.
A small moment, but one my daughter and I will always remember.

With Ritesh Banglani, a prominent Indian venture capital investor in Bangalore – in a café where pitch decks usually rule the conversation, our table was all cricket.

CHAPTER 3

BOXING DAY TEST, MELBOURNE

Day 1

Melbourne Cricket Ground on the morning of the 26th was buzzing with people. Taking in all that chaos from the cab, though, I felt still. A different kind of stillness – more like a buzz of reverence that only comes from everyone recognising that something major is coming.

Three separate trams hissed around the stadium, fans chattered and the smell of sunscreen and meat pies was already in the air. Kids with small cricket bats weaved between grown-ups. A few of those adults were wearing Santa hats over their Aussie caps – a reminder that it was still technically the holiday season.

I was dying of excitement, so much so that I didn't even bother checking into the hotel room and made my way straight to the stadium instead. Even in the cab to the ground I knew it wasn't the ideal decision. I had enough time to freshen up before attending the match but the child in me just wouldn't listen. I don't blame him, even the adult in me wouldn't have forgiven myself if I missed a minute of the match because I chose to go to my room beforehand. Anyway, I got out of the cab and as soon as I stepped out, the cab driver drove away. That was good and all, I'd paid via the app already, but there was a tiny little problem. My suitcase was still inside the car.

My heart dropped. What if I missed the first ball? Yes, that's what I was worried about the most. Not the fact that I'd lose clothes, or that my laptop was in there, but that I would miss the first ball of this glorious event. In a panic, I chased him. To the best of my ability, at least, which quickly proved to be insufficient. I only caught up with him when security realised I was chasing him and stopped the cab. The driver seemed pretty nonchalant about the issue. It hardly mattered to me. I was simply relieved there would be no match-missing, though my back was not thanking me after all that impromptu running.

The line at the gate moved fast and within minutes I was inside. And that's when it hit me – the Melbourne Cricket Ground wasn't just big; it was monumental. A hundred thousand seats spread around a vast green field that looked like a sacred space. You see glimpses of the MCG on TV, sure. You know the numbers, the history, the statues around the stadium. (Shane Warne's is my favourite.) But walking into it, seeing the stands curve into the sky, is something else entirely, and it overwhelms you in the best possible way.

I remember thinking, *This place is too good to be real.* And yet, it functioned like clockwork. Cloakrooms for bags, spotless toilets despite the crowd, food stalls every few rows so you never had to miss a ball for a hot dog. It was engineered for joy, which is how it should be. The stalls reminded me that I hadn't eaten since that morning, which got me to think about how well engineered the place was.

A few minutes of fanboying and I reached my seat – M20-something in the second lowest stand. Being lower down meant there was a bit of covering above, but despite this, I had a pretty great view of the opening day and was quietly thanking my stars – and that security guard who stopped the taxi – for getting me in. Little did I know the views would only get better over the next few days.

I sat down for a few minutes, chatting with my seat neighbour for the day. Can't remember much about him except that he politely listened while I went off on a minor rant about the Indian national anthem. Let me grace you with the same rant.

See, I studied at a Sainik School growing up. *Sainik* is the Hindi word for soldier, and these schools specifically train young boys to join the defence academies. As you might expect, it was the kind of place where you're taught to march, salute and sing the anthem as it was meant to be sung: in exactly fifty-two seconds. It's something that's been drilled into me so deeply that I can't help but notice when people take, let's say … creative liberties.

Guess how many seconds the national anthem at the MCG was sung for? (Spoiler: way more than fifty-two seconds.)

While I still stubbornly ranted with my neighbour, it didn't really matter as much as it usually would because I was also left dazed by the vibrations of tens of thousands of people singing the same tune together. You can't catch that on TV. Not the sound, not the feeling, and definitely not the goosebumps. On TV they show the players or a few crowd shots. But when you're in the crowd, surrounded by thousands of voices in unison, it's something else entirely. In that moment, there's no way anyone could not feel like they belonged.

...

A few minutes later, the players started walking onto the ground. Australia had won the toss and elected to bat – a good decision by skipper Pat Cummins. On a side note, every time a captain elects to bat after winning the toss I'm reminded of a funny but reasonably true quote:

> *'When you win the toss – bat. If you are in doubt, think about it, then bat. If you have very big doubts, consult a colleague then bat.' – W G Grace*

Grace was a prominent batting all-rounder in the late nineteenth century and is heralded as the father of modern batsmanship. While the times have certainly changed since his days, especially with the way pitches are maintained, his advice to always bat first generally works well.

On another funny note, here's a quip I read a few years ago: If you gave a low target, you should have batted better. If you got a high target, you should have picked batting, you fool. While this is a joke, it sums up nicely the advice of armchair cricketers. (Don't worry, I'm guilty of giving that same analysis.)

Usman Khawaja and Sam Konstas walked onto the field filled with eleven Indian players and I couldn't take my eyes off them. Clearly, I wasn't the only one. The roar from the Aussie crowd said it all – there was some serious buzz around this debut. I was hyped for this kid too – nineteen years old and his first Test cap. (I mean, he did play the Prime Minister's XI warm-up matches against India, but never in front of this kind of crowd.)

On top of that, many were questioning the selectors' decision to replace Nathan McSweeney with this young boy. Sure, McSweeney wasn't the right opener for the team either. He was pushed to open for the team while not being a regular opener. Against an attack like Bumrah's, that doesn't go well. Still, there wasn't much evidence to suggest that Konstas would fare the other way. But looking at him walk out, you could feel something shift. This lad was already carrying the quiet, collective hope of a nation looking for its next legendary opener.

His first few minutes didn't scream legendary though. He looked jittery – extravagant, even – and it didn't come off. The Test cricket purist in me would have appreciated some elegant defence, but that didn't seem like his style. I said to myself, *Well, you're only a nineteen year old once, might as well make use of that youthful fire.*

At one point, he was 5 off 21 balls and playing shots that looked like they belonged more in a T20 highlights reel than a Boxing Day Test. He played wild swings and risky reverse scoops that only looked good when they paid off. And just when I thought they wouldn't, they did. I couldn't believe it – he scooped Bumrah for a four, then immediately a six, and simply didn't stop! I swear it felt like he took Bumrah to the line every over.

Within a few overs, he went from a talented teenager to looking like he owned the place. And by the time he got out at 60 in 65 balls (an insanely good strike rate), he'd done a lot of damage to the Indians. Not just to their bowling figures, but their morale as well. You could see it in their body language. You know how commentators say the shoulders are dropping, or India looks tired? This time, they actually were. From the stands, you could feel it. Bumrah looked frustrated, the fielders looked flat, and there was more relief than happiness on the ground.

For a session and a bit, this teenager had bulldozed one of the world's best bowlers (and India's best hope). As he walked into the stands, even the Indians in the crowd didn't cheer as loudly as we usually did.

Normally, we'd be up on our feet the moment a guy like that got out and cheered for the wicket. This time too, we were indeed on our feet, but instead of cheering for the wicket, we were wholeheartedly applauding the innings he'd played.

As for me, I stood and clapped a bit longer than the rest, knowing I'd just witnessed something rare – one of those moments you tell your kids about. In two decades, near the end of this young gentleman's career, I know I will be saying this: I was there. At the Melbourne Cricket Ground. On the first morning of the Boxing Day Test. When Sam Konstas announced himself to the world. I. WAS. THERE.

As the applause died down, I sat and did what every cricket fan does when something this momentous happens – pulled out my phone and started texting people about it. The first on the list to get my messages was Monil, my cousin Janhavi's husband and a fellow passionate cricket fan. He used to live in Sydney, played competitive grade cricket on the North Shore, and even after moving back to India, he still wakes up at 4.30 am just to catch these games live. I was damn sure he'd be doing just that as I sent him a few photos of the ground. Soon enough he replied with, 'Thanks for the pics. This is making me miss Australia even more.'

There were others too – friends, college groups, Twitter DMs. Yes, Twitter DMs. (I still can't quite call it X). I made a new connection in India due to this series – Ritesh Banglani, a partner at Stellaris Venture Partners, one of India's leading venture capital (VC) firms. I connected with him through his tweet that mentioned how he couldn't attend the series as he planned to, and was selling his tickets. I offered to take the tickets off his hands, and out of that, another connection formed. It struck me how the love for this sport brought two people 8,000 kilometres apart into a conversation that felt like we'd been talking cricket for years. This game really is something else.

Sanjay Swamy was another. A well-known name in Indian startup circles and a serious cricket nut. We'd exchanged notes before but this series brought a new kind of energy into our conversations.

One interesting thing I've noticed about highly accomplished people, especially in the Indian VC space, is that no matter how packed their lives are, they always seem to make room for one passion. And for many of them, that passion is cricket. Not casually either, they do it properly. Scorecards, line-ups, squad analysis, pitch conditions. This game doesn't just unite nations. It builds unlikely friendships too.

Oh, and just an hour later, my cousin Janhavi texts me this: 'Hi Nikhil *Anna* (brother in South Indian languages), how are you doing? I heard you're having a great time attending the matches. And someone is very jealous.'

She didn't have to say who; Monil had clearly been talking about it non-stop. I smiled. Somehow, even from halfway around the world, cricket still found a way to connect us.

Something else caught my attention during the match: the whole place exuded the culture of cricket. For example: At 3.50 pm, just after the final session began, the entire stadium stood up and tipped their hats in honour of Shane Warne. Some did it quietly. Others, especially in Bay 13, waved theirs like they were trying to signal a rescue chopper. Imagine that – ninety thousand people either tipping their hat or supporting the act at the exact same time. It was symbolic, sure, but it was also deeply moving. A minute later, someone in the crowd loudly cheered, 'Go Warneyyyy!', and I couldn't help but smile at the love and passion with which the community celebrated one of its own in a way only this sport can.

After that, the play settled into a classic Test match rhythm. Australia reached 311 for 6 by stumps. Steve Smith was still standing, which as any Indian fan knows, is never a great sign. It wasn't a disaster for India, but it wasn't exactly a win either. Let's just say we'd seen worse.

...

As I came out of the stadium after the final session, I was tired. So tired, in fact, that the first thing I did when I reached my hotel room was crash on the bed and regain my senses. Even as I slept, I knew I didn't have much time to spare. In less than an hour, I had to be at the Boxing Day Gala at the National Gallery of Victoria (NGV).

The Yayoi Kusama art exhibition was running there at the time. I hadn't even heard of the event until a few days earlier. Now here I was with an invite to this exclusive gathering. All thanks to Cal McGuirk, a senior executive at the Centre for Australia–India Relations (CAIR).

I first met Cal at one of the AIYD events where we'd exchanged a few words, and later connected on LinkedIn. CAIR has been a major driver of the Australia–India connection lately; not just in policy or trade, but in sport, culture and everyday people stuff. They'd hosted a major sports innovation summit in Brisbane, but I couldn't make it, so I sent Cal a quick message, just to ask if anything else was planned for Melbourne. No expectations. To my surprise, he replied with a quiet little gem – a Boxing Day gala at the NGV, paired with the chance to experience the Yayoi Kusama exhibition. No posters. No public RSVP links. Just an invite sitting quietly in my inbox, because I happened to ask. Thank you again, Cal.

Back to the exhibition. I'm not what you'd call naturally artsy. I don't pretend to know what brushstrokes mean or why dots matter, but there was something about Yayoi Kusama's work that pulled me in anyway. You see, she painted what you'd call traditional paintings. Think big canvases covered in lines and dots. But what she's best known for are her infinity rooms. Entire rooms covered in bright dots, mirrors, lights, or a combination of all three. She makes art an immersive experience. Some of it felt playful. Some of it felt oddly meditative.

One installation in particular, a room full of paper flowers, made me pause. I don't know if that was the point, but it made me think about how we reflect the world around us, whether we mean to or not. Maybe that's what art's supposed to do – trick you into thinking deeper thoughts without warning.

The exhibition was followed by a reception that brought together people from across the Australia–India bilateral space. For me, it was a mix of familiar faces and new ones. I ended up chatting with the then assistant minister for foreign affairs Tim Watts, who's also an AIYD alumnus. Naturally, the conversation veered to cricket. He mentioned Steve Smith's century and how strong the Aussie team looked heading into Day 2, with genuine excitement both for the game and Australia-India relations.

Sometime during the exhibition, I found myself standing next to Nick Hockley, the then CEO of Cricket Australia, when both of us paused in front of one of Kusama's infinity installations. He's not a household name, but for someone who's followed the game as long and as closely as I have, he's a significant figure. It's not every day you run into the CEO of Cricket Australia in a room full of polka dots. The day had been excellent for both of us – a fantastic Day 1 at the MCG by all accounts.

He was the organiser-in-chief and I had soaked in every moment of it.

The conversation that followed was truly memorable too. A lot of that credit goes to Nick. He was warm, open and genuinely enthusiastic, especially as our chat shifted from Kusama's dots to the day's play at the MCG. I complimented him and the Cricket Australia team for providing us fans with great cricket experiences. And when I mentioned that I'd done the Daughters and Dads program, his face lit up. 'I did that too,' he said, smiling. Just like that, the chat turned easy. We swapped stories, compared notes, and I even showed him a few photos from our session. As it turned out, we'd both had the same coach-facilitator. That little coincidence gave the moment a weirdly personal touch. As a fan, I felt very looked after, especially as this conversation and watching him talk about the game with so much passion made me realise that that care came in abundance from the very top. If you're reading this, thanks a lot for that chat, Nick.

I ran into other wonderful people in the latter half of the night, including the kabaddi team representing India in the match I'd end up attending a few days later, but my social battery quickly ran out and I left the venue by 9.30 that night.

By the time I reached my room, I wasn't thinking in full sentences anymore. My feet hurt. My head was still buzzing, part cricket, part Kusama, part conversations I hadn't quite processed yet. Somewhere between the teenage debut at the G, a polka-dotted gallery full of diplomats and CEOs and swapping stories with the head of Cricket Australia, I'd packed a week's worth of emotion into a single day. All I could do was lie flat, stare at the ceiling for a minute, and smile to myself. What a start to Melbourne.

Day 2

If Day 1 was a sprint, Day 2 was more a deep breath. I woke up feeling like I'd spent twenty-four hours in a highlight reel. The suitcase drama, Konstas's innings, the crowd, the art exhibition, a chat with the Cricket Australia CEO – my brain felt full and my legs were sore. I'd seen enough chaos. Today, I just wanted to sit with the game, not chase it. So, I slowed down.

The play had already begun by the time I entered the ground, and for the first time on this trip, I didn't mind missing a few overs. As I entered the stands, I heard the crowd roar at a boundary, and all the aches I came to the ground with evaporated instantly. Upon taking my seat, I noticed the Indian players wearing black armbands. That symbolism only meant one thing – someone important had passed away. A quick Google revealed it was the late Dr Manmohan Singh, ex-prime minister of India. God bless his soul.

While it wasn't the best news to start my day with, the armbands only made me appreciate the culture of the sport even more. Let me tell you how. Cricket, as a sport, is a world of its own. Sure, there are the occasional politics and rumours that link the world outside with the game, but on a day-to-day basis, there's so much happening within the game – from updates about players to sponsor drama – that it's easy to get caught up in it all and forget to look beyond it. That's why gestures like the black armband honouring a national leader of the past show that after all is said and done, the players haven't lost sight of the fact this is just a game, and there's an entire world that exists outside of it and functions independently of them.

Like I said, Day 2 became all about the atmosphere, the spirit, the ambience of the ground. I stepped back and took it all in. I don't remember much about the play, but that's not to say it wasn't memorable. It's just that the match took a back seat as I decided to simply exist in the beauty of everything that was happening around me.

It was a beautiful sunlit day, so I took a stroll around the stadium during lunch and checked out the legendary statues all around the ground. There's something about those walks in between overs and innings that remind you cricket isn't just about what's happening on the pitch. It's everything around it. The rituals, the people, the memory. Those sixteen statues, standing silently as the crowds pass by, are living proof. They show that what brings people back year after year isn't just runs or wickets. It's culture. And cricket, more than most sports, knows how to hold onto it.

For those who aren't well-versed in the lore of these statues, look at the list below; if a name catches your eye, maybe read up on them a little. They're all great men and women who deserve every ounce of attention we can pay them.

Legends enshrined in bronze
Sir Donald Bradman (cricket)
Shane Warne (cricket)
Dennis Lillee (cricket)
Bill Ponsford (cricket)
Keith Miller (cricket)
Neil Harvey (cricket)
Shirley Strickland (athletics)
Betty Cuthbert (athletics)

Ron Barassi (Australian Rules Football)
Leigh Matthews (Australian Rules Football)
Dick Reynolds (Australian Rules Football)
Haydn Bunton Sr (Australian Rules Football)
Norm Smith (Australian Rules Football)
John Coleman (Australian Rules Football)
Jim Stynes (Australian Rules Football)
Kevin Bartlett (Australian Rules Football)

I'll be honest, I didn't know the stories behind many of them until I found myself wandering past their bronzed likenesses. There's something about seeing them up close, out there in the open air, that nudges you into curiosity. And once you start reading, it's hard not to get drawn in. These aren't just names; they're chapters in Australia's sporting history, quietly waiting for someone to stop and take notice.

That's the beauty of showing up in person. The TV gives you the angles, the stats, the analysis. But the stadium gives you everything else – the pause, the wandering, the side stories that sneak up on you while you're looking for coffee or stretching your legs. You stumble upon greatness, sometimes literally. And in moments like that, the game almost becomes secondary because you realise that the sport isn't only played on the field. It's lived in the footsteps around it.

At one point, I wandered in the stadium to a Shane Warne Legacy Health Check clinic, a small stall with a self-serve style health check machine and a life-size cut-out of Shane Warne in his classic hat-tipping pose. His family and close associates have set it up as a small but powerful way to carry forward his legacy, turning a public health message into something personal. Observing the atmosphere around the stall, with hundreds of fans queuing up to check their heart rate and other health metrics, I realised how uniquely Australian the whole concept is. Dignified, yet playful, just like Warney.

Inside the stadium, the crowd did a Mexican wave. I too jumped up with the rest, arms in the air, cheering like a kid at recess.

After the final session, I walked out of the stadium with a sense of fulfilment about the day. Unlike the day before, there was no drama today – just good cricket and some space to think. But Melbourne, as always, wasn't done with me yet.

...

By the time I left my hotel room, an hour after the match finished, the city had completely changed gears. The noise of the crowd was gone, replaced by the usual end-of-working-day hum; trams clanking, people heading to dinner, that sort of thing. In fact, I was heading to dinner too, with a friend and a fellow delegate from my AIYD delegation, Drew Ambrose.

Drew is one of those people who's done a lot but never makes a big deal about it. He's an investigative journalist with Al Jazeera, the kind who doesn't just cover stories, but goes wherever they're unfolding. Earthquakes, refugee crises, political coups; you name it, he's probably reported on it. He's lived in Jakarta and Kuala Lumpur, speaks Indonesian fluently, and has this easy, thoughtful way of carrying all that experience without ever needing to tell you how much he's seen. You just pick it up in the way he listens – fully, curiously. And the way he always seems to know the most interesting place on any block.

I first came across Drew on LinkedIn, right after the AIYD announced its 2024 cohort. Both Drew and I were part of the Australian delegation.

He'd shared the announcement with a tongue-in-cheek caption about how, now that he was nearing forty, this was technically his final year of eligibility. It was a light-hearted post, but it struck a chord with me. I wasn't exactly fresh out of college myself, so I sent him a quick, 'Ha ha, good one,' and a connection formed.

We met a few months later during the AIYD delegation in Canberra and Sydney, and hit it off properly. Later that year I dropped a message in the AIYD WhatsApp group saying I'd be in Melbourne for the Test. Drew responded saying he'd be there too. Naturally, we made plans to catch up.

So there I was, a few weeks later, standing outside a barely marked doorway off Malthouse Lane. The kind of place you'd only know about if someone like Drew told you to find it. From the outside, it looked more like a service entrance than anything else. No board, no sign, no music – just a door left ajar that looked like it might lead to a storeroom. Drew walked out of that door and took me inside, where it was a whole different story. Dim lights, polished timber and bartenders who looked like they loved their job. All of it made me feel like I'd just stepped into a better version of my evening. We found a spot near the bar, which by now I knew was called Eau De Vie, and looking at the menu, I simply handed all control over to my waiter. I had no idea what was on the menu and wasn't going to pressure myself to figure it out. All the bartender got from me was, 'You make what you think I should be drinking tonight.'

In all honesty, I'm proud of doing that. A few years ago, this used to stress me out. Walking into fancy places where I couldn't pronounce half the items, where the menu looked like it was written in French, and everyone else seemed to know what they were doing. Part of it is being an immigrant. You arrive in a new country and you're not just trying to understand the rules, you're trying to look like you already know them. There's this constant, low-key pressure to blend in. You don't want to be the one holding up the line, mispronouncing something basic, or asking someone to repeat what they said because you couldn't catch their accent.

I've felt that awkwardness in restaurants, on public transport, even while buying coffee. You learn quickly which questions are okay to ask and which ones you pretend you already know the answer to. But somewhere along the way, I let go of that. Maybe it's age, exhaustion, or that I now know more things and can make my way around these situations that makes me realise there's nothing wrong with not knowing, and you don't have to understand everything to feel like you belong.

At the bar, cutting through the noise, I was drawn into fascinating stories from Drew about his work in investigative journalism. He spoke of the incredible experiences he's had and the remarkable people he's met over the years – from interviewing heads of state to navigating immense challenges in pursuit of the truth. Drew is a natural storyteller, and it's no surprise he's become the accomplished journalist he is today.

From the bar, we made our way to Supernormal for dinner. The food was great, the place was lively, and it had that comfortable buzz you only get when the energy of a city winds down. After that, we headed to another spot – this man just wouldn't stop showing me the city. Drew was meeting a few of his colleagues and friends, but my social battery was running out, so I only stayed briefly. I said my goodbyes, thanked Drew for the night, and made my way back to the hotel. It had been a slow but full day of cricket, legacy, drinks, conversation. I couldn't have asked for a better way to end it.

Day 3

They say you need to have strong opinions, loosely held. But there's a strong opinion I hold very strongly. And it's that the cloakroom at the MCG deserves its own shout-out.

Day 3 only proved me right.

See, I had a slightly fancier evening ahead of me, and I needed a blazer for it. Instead of heading back to the hotel after the cricket, I figured I'd just stash my formalwear at the stadium. In most places, that would've meant shoving it into my bag and spending the rest of the day delicately carrying it around like a newborn baby (minus the crying, plus the wrinkling).

Not here, though.

'Sir, you have a blazer?'

'Yes.'

'Let me get you a hanger. Give me a minute.'

That's what the cloakroom attendant actually said, and I was in love. Imagine that. A proper hanger. At a cricket ground. For one blazer. I half expected them to pull out an ironing board and ask if I wanted it lightly steamed.

Maybe I should have been used to being surprised, because it was becoming a theme on this trip. Every time I expected things to get messy, Australia handed me comfort. Whether that was cloakrooms with hangers or toilets that still smelled like lemon by evening, the little things kept showing up. I've travelled enough to know that's rare.

And so, with my jacket safely stashed, I made my way into the stadium. The play had just started. My body was definitely asking for a break after two packed days, but my brain had other plans. Today was Bay 13.

Now, before I go any further, a quick explainer for those who haven't spent their lives obsessing over cricket stadium layouts.

Bay 13 is a seating section at the Melbourne Cricket Ground. Not just any section, it's the wild child of the MCG – it's where chants mutate into roars, where the noise never just passes through but comes back amplified. Imagine grown-ups who spend weekdays in suits turning up as Mario, kangaroos or bananas, and a crowd that cheers someone getting escorted out for rowdy behaviour almost as much as a fallen wicket. The whole bay hums with that kind of reckless energy that's loud and chaotic, but charming in a very innocent way.

The chants here are relentless, the beer snakes are legendary, and the vibe is completely unfiltered. I once heard a theory on why that is. For one, Bay 13 is directly opposite the Members Pavilion, which has the most expensive seats in the stadium. While Bay 13 has a similar view (because the bowlers change sides every over), it also takes the full brunt of the sun, forcing people to hydrate themselves with, you guessed it, chilled beer. Moreover, it's no more expensive than the rest of the general admission bays, so anyone who wants an amazing view and is willing to drown out the sunlight in beer actively books this spot.

That's just a theory, though. I say that because it's garnered the name of being a rowdy area, so the fame surrounding it acts like a self-fulfilling prophecy, attracting folk who want to fulfil it.

That reputation also means security is never too far away. Bay 13 might be general admission but it's treated like the front row at a rock concert. Security guards patrol the aisles like hawks. There are stern looks, no small talk and a quiet readiness that says, 'Please don't make me do my job.'

And that brings me to *him*. The most serious security guard I've ever seen. Not just in a stadium. Anywhere. You'd think he was guarding the gold vault at Fort Knox. Buzz cut, tight black t-shirt, dark glasses despite the clouds, and absolutely no hint of emotion. He stood at the entrance to the bay and purposefully shot everyone a don't-you-dare-mess-around look that made me think he took his job way too seriously.

Stepping into the arena, though, the look didn't seem unnecessary anymore. The bay was exactly like I imagined it would be – a cricket-themed carnival where the game was only half the attraction. It hadn't even been an hour since the game started and there was already a small beer snake making its way around the place.

Some people might call this kind of thing a nuisance. They'll say it blocks the view, spills beer, gets rowdy. I get that. But to me, it never felt like Bay 13 was trying to ruin anyone's day. If anything, it was trying to make sure everyone had a good one. This wasn't a frat party gone wrong. It was a ritual that came with its own unspoken code. You could tell who was in on the code too. You passed cups down to add to the beer snake when someone tapped you on the shoulder. You joined the chant if it reached your row. You knew when to boo the people who didn't stand for the wave. You knew when to laugh and when to move aside for security. It was messy, but never malicious.

India began the day at 164 for 5, still trailing by over 300 runs, and things weren't looking great. It wasn't a total collapse, but the tension was thick. Every dot ball felt heavier, every appeal louder, and every dismissal a little more deflating. Australia had put up a massive first innings total and the scoreboard pressure was starting to show. The kind of slow, tightening grip that Test cricket is ruthless for. It was the sort of situation where survival starts to feel like a small victory, and anything more feels like wishful thinking. After Rishabh Pant's wicket at 191, the situation seemed even worse.

Only much later did I realise that while all this was unfolding on the field, Sunil Gavaskar had gone on air and called Pant's shot 'stupid, stupid, stupid'. It had become a whole thing by the time I checked my phone that night. Debates, reactions, memes. I hadn't heard the comment live, of course. That's the thing about being in the stadium – you're entirely in the moment, but you also miss a lot of what's being said *about* the moment.

And yet, I wouldn't trade it.

Sure, you miss the sharp analysis, the slow-motion replays, the hot mics and the viral gaffes. But what you get instead is something commentary can't quite replicate, which is the raw pulse of a match shared with tens of thousands around you. That collective groan when a wicket falls. The weird silence that spreads when a batter reviews a close LBW. The hopeful murmur before the third umpire's decision. You feel the match more than you follow it.

It's funny. From the stands, I didn't think much of Pant's dismissal in the moment. It was frustrating, yeah, but also in character. Rishabh Pant has always batted like he's trying to bend the laws of Test cricket out of shape. Sometimes it works, sometimes it doesn't. But it's never boring. Gavaskar's words, though, reminded me how often we confuse disappointment for certainty. We want players to be consistent, mature, dependable, but not dull. We praise instinct when it succeeds and scold it when it fails. And we do all this from the comfort of hindsight.

In the end, it didn't matter whether the shot was smart or stupid. What mattered was that something stirred after that moment. Nitish Kumar Reddy, the twenty-two-year-old all-rounder, walked in.

I was already bracing for the worst when Nitish walked to the crease. At that point, I'd more or less written the day off. India was six down, the sky looked moody, and I was convinced the match was crawling toward a rain-soaked draw.

Lunch had been a bright spot, though. I met up with Aman Gaur, and we had a good catch-up while walking around the ground. It was the kind of relaxed conversation that resets your day a bit, regardless of what's happening on the field.

I first met Aman during my time with the AIYD delegation, where he was part of the steering committee, the team that organises and leads the dialogue. Aman led the sports-focused sessions, including a memorable AFL game at Manuka Oval in Canberra, which still stands out as a highlight. AIYD isn't necessarily well known outside its circle, but once you're part of it, you realise just how strong and diverse the network is. It includes Grammy-winning musicians, leading journalists and politicians in prominent positions across both countries. It's a community that stays connected well beyond the delegation itself.

Drew hadn't been the only one to reply to my message in the AIYD WhatsApp group. Aman responded too, and we made plans to meet at the MCG during the Boxing Day Test. I'd brought along a cricket book by Gideon Haigh as a gift to him, and we chatted about growing up with cricket in Australia, his work in law and public policy, and his plans to run for local council. He was also headed to an event later that day that I was attending too, so we planned to catch up again. It was a solid, thoughtful conversation, the kind that stays with you.

And then, back in the stands, the mood started to shift. Nitish began swinging. Not recklessly, but with a kind of quiet confidence that made you sit up straighter in your seat. He built a solid partnership with Washington Sundar, and just when the crowd was getting into it, the rain arrived. By then, though, Nitish had already lit a spark. When play resumed, he picked up right where he left off, steering the innings with composure through four different partnerships, ending the day on the last wicket. By stumps, India was 358 for 9 – still trailing by 116 runs, but with Reddy unbeaten on 105, the day had turned out far better than expected.

...

As the players walked off and the crowd began to thin, I made my way toward the exit but not out of the stadium just yet. That blazer I'd dropped off at the cloakroom in the morning? It was time to put it to use. The cricket may have been over for the day, but Melbourne still had plans for me. Next stop: John Cain Arena. Kabaddi night.

It wasn't far, probably a few minutes from the stadium exit, and by the time I got there, the sun had just dipped behind the skyline. I'd scored a VIP pass by following up one of those you-should-definitely-come conversations from earlier in the week at the Boxing Day gala at the NGV.

Kabaddi, if you've never seen it, is the kind of sport that makes you sit up before you even understand the rules. One player charges into enemy territory, touches as many defenders as they can, and tries to make it back before they slam the raider into the floor. Traditionally, to add to the tension, the raider's supposed to do all this while holding their breath (a rule that's more symbolic now). And the whole match? Done in about forty minutes. No slow build-up, no pacing yourself. It's fast, theatrical and over before you know it. It's like professional tag had a baby with street-side wrestling.

I walked up to the VIP gate ticket in hand only to be stopped before I could say a word. 'General entry's that way,' the security guard said, already pointing me toward another line. He hadn't even looked at the pass. Just took one look at me, even blazer and all, and decided I didn't belong. I paused, smiled and explained I had a VIP ticket. He glanced down, saw the ticket, nodded once and stepped aside without a fuss. No big deal. Just a man doing his job. But as I walked through, I couldn't help but laugh a little. I was feeling sharp in that blazer, but still got redirected like I was trying my luck. It was a small thing that was over in seconds, but it reminded me that sometimes, even when you're exactly where you're supposed to be, you still have to say it out loud.

The place was buzzing, and not in a polite, indoor-sport kind of way. This was full-volume, high-energy and unapologetically Indian. The match hadn't started yet but the arena already felt alive. Bollywood beats pulsed through the speakers giving the whole space a pre-show heartbeat. Spotlights circled slowly over the yellow and red mat at the centre, as if trying to make it feel even more like a stage. The seating was steadily filling up, and the closer I got to the VIP section, the more I felt like I was stepping into something a little special. There weren't chants yet, just a kind of warm murmur with people arriving, talking, scanning the program and taking their seats with a casual but growing excitement. I slid into mine, only a few rows from the edge of the court. It was close enough to feel like you'd be pulled into the game if you leaned forward too much. The lights, the music, the crowd, it was all holding its breath. And so was I.

Before the match began, there was a proper inauguration ceremony with speeches from dignitaries, acknowledgements of the event's significance, and a chance for everyone in the VIP stands to meet and connect more formally. It almost felt like a mini AIYD reunion with many of my program's alumni and cohort mates there to watch the match along with me.

One of them was Arth Tuteja, whom I met at my AIYD delegation. He was as sharp as ever, always somewhere at the intersection of politics, policy and good food. He works closely with Tim Watts who, like I mentioned, is also an AIYD alum. Arth also mentioned that his father ran an Indian restaurant in the city, which, of course, immediately went on my list. I'd been craving a proper Indian meal, and honestly, where better to go than a place with AIYD pedigree and actual family ties to the kitchen?

The opening ceremony lasted for about half an hour before everyone started to head back to their seats. From mine, I had a clear, close-up view of the action – and what action it was. The match itself was a whirlwind. India was playing against an Aussie team made up of some AFL stars. It was fast-paced, loud and incredibly physical. You could feel the tension each time a raider crossed the line, trying to tag someone and rush back without getting tackled. I hadn't watched a kabaddi match in the longest time, and sometimes I couldn't figure out who won the round and why, but I was still incredibly involved in the game.

The environment had a part to play in this too. The whole set-up felt like something straight out of the Indian Pro Kabaddi League – bright lights, booming commentary, dramatic intros. They'd even flown down the same presenters from India, and it showed. The lights and music amplified every tackle and raid; the whole thing made for television.

And then came cricketing stars Irfan Pathan and Shane Watson, and Jatin Sapru, the popular cricket broadcaster. They were at the event to give kabaddi a boost, and their seats were right beside mine before they were to head on-air during halftime. I wasn't about to pester them mid-prep, but when the moment felt right, when the moment presented itself, I asked for a quick photo. They were warm and gracious about it.

Not much of a conversation, but just enough to leave me grinning. I mean, what are the chances you'll find yourself seated next to such famous personalities, in a kabaddi match of all places? This was a trip that just kept giving and I was gladly accepting everything it gave me.

The match itself wasn't exactly close. The Indian team, made up of retired pros, pretty much cruised through. But for me, the real highlight wasn't the score. I hadn't watched a proper kabaddi match in years, and seeing it play out under the bright lights of John Cain Arena with full production, broadcast cameras and a packed stadium felt surreal. It was the same sport I remembered from dusty schoolyards back home, just sharper, faster, louder. Somehow, it felt both familiar and completely new.

After the match, I made my way to Desi Dhaba, the Indian restaurant that Arth's dad ran right in the heart of the city. The place was lively, even at that hour, with the kind of warmth you don't need to be a regular to feel. As soon as I sat down, I asked one of the staff if Arth was around. The waiter paused for a second, confused. Then his face lit up. 'Ohh, you mean Golu Bhaiya?' he said, laughing. Of course. Every Indian family has that one nickname. The one that never makes it to a resume but sticks for life. Turns out, no one at the restaurant called him Arth. Just Golu Bhaiya. And somehow, that made the whole place feel even more familiar.

I pulled out my phone and messaged him, asking what I should order. He replied right away with a few suggestions and I went with his top pick. A few minutes later, before anything else hit the table, a tall glass of chilled lassi arrived. The waiter smiled and said, 'This is from Arth,' before walking off. I hadn't asked for it, and Arth hadn't mentioned it either, it just showed up, unannounced and perfect. I messaged him a quick thank you. He just replied, 'Welcome'. Simple. Thoughtful. No big moment, just the kind of gesture that lands exactly the way it should.

By the time I left Desi Dhaba I had a full tummy but nothing was left in the energy department. I made my way straight back to the hotel and crashed. It was the kind of tiredness that doesn't come from one thing, but everything at once. The matches, the movement, the moments that kept stacking up across three unforgettable days.

On the field, the Test had finally found its rhythm. Day 1 belonged to Australia with some top-tier batting. Day 2 drifted a little. But Day 3? That's when the match came alive. India clawed back into the game with Nitish Kumar Reddy and Washington Sundar putting on a show. It was classic Test cricket, the kind that unfolds slowly, rewards patience, and then suddenly demands your full attention.

And then there was everything beyond the match itself. Every evening seemed to bring someone new – a dinner, a chat, a familiar face from the AIYD network. One night it was a catch-up with Drew Ambrose, another, an event where I got to meet Nick Hockley. Cricket was the anchor but the week had its own rhythm – part sport, part adventure.

By the time I reached my room I could barely move, but I still recorded a short video for my daughter. Just a simple check-in, a wave, a smile. Enough to stay close across the distance. The past three days had left me completely spent, but somehow, completely content too.

Day 4

There are seats you chase, and there are seats that reward you for showing up. P20, Row A, Seat 11 was the latter.

It was one of those mornings where everything aligned without fuss. I woke up early, slipped into something warm and made my way to the G with a quiet sort of anticipation. No adrenaline, no chaos – just that slow-building buzz you feel when you know you're about to witness something special. From the moment I sat down, I knew this one was different. Slightly elevated, tucked at just the right angle behind the bowler's arm, it offered a panoramic sweep of the MCG that felt like a director's cut of the game. I could see everything. The batter's stance, the bowler's approach, the exact shape of the field, right down to the square leg's shuffle between deliveries. The noise and chaos of Bay 13 felt a world away, replaced here by a quieter, more contemplative rhythm. It wasn't just a seat; it was a perspective.

I didn't move for the rest of the day. Not even to stretch my legs. For hours I just sat, completely absorbed, watching every ball, every shift in tension, every little drama play out below. At that moment, I felt like I'd arrived. Not in some grand, career-defining way, but in a quieter, more personal sense. It felt like the kind of view that rewards years of being a cricket fanatic. Like the universe had quietly whispered, 'This one's for you, enjoy it.'

From my seat in P20 I watched as the last bit of India's first innings wrapped up. Nitish Kumar Reddy was gone before most people had even settled in with their coffee (or beer, perhaps, given the warm weather). One mistimed drive, one catch, and just like that, the innings was over. It felt abrupt, the kind of finish that leaves you blinking at the scoreboard thinking, 'Wait, that's it?'

Australia was ahead by 105 and within minutes the second innings was underway. It's funny how fast the mood inside a stadium can flip. One moment it's end-of-innings applause, the next you're watching Sam

Konstas mark his guard again and everyone's sitting a little straighter. Half the match was behind us, but you could feel the mood beginning to stir.

There were still two full days left, but with clouds lurking in the forecast, people around me had already started whispering about how much play we'd actually get. If anything, it made things a bit more interesting. Not necessarily tense, just uncertain enough to keep everyone guessing. Personally, I've never seen rain as a bad thing in Test cricket. Sure, it's frustrating when you're in the stands and play gets stopped, but it also throws a bit of spice into the match. Suddenly, both teams have to think differently. A bit of rain on Day 4? That could mean both captains quietly agree to speed things up the next day. One team might declare after hitting a quick hundred, the other might promote a pinch-hitter just to keep the scoreboard moving. No one wants a draw, especially after three and a half days of hard-fought cricket. So, in a weird way, the weather can force everyone to be more creative.

As the second innings played out I found myself moonlighting as the unofficial weatherman for a whole bunch of friends back in India. Most of them were watching live streams while half-asleep in their beds, trying to decide if the match was worth staying up for. So my phone kept buzzing with questions: 'Is it raining yet?', 'Will we get a full session?', 'Should I stay up or sleep?'

I'd glance up at the sky, pull out my phone and fire off updates like I was on Cricket Australia's payroll. Sometimes I'd stand up slightly, just to check how many umbrellas were opening in the lower seats. 'Bit of drizzle, but clearing up,' I'd write. Or, 'Looks like a full final session is coming up.' It became a running thread throughout the day and, honestly, kept me even more tuned into both the match and the way others were living it vicariously through me.

As the day wore on, the ambience inside the MCG began to shift. It wasn't the loud, electric kind of shift you feel when a team's on a roll or a player's racing toward a century. This was something slower, more gradual. The sort of change you only really notice because you've been sitting still long enough to catch it. People around me weren't shouting or chanting anymore. They were watching. Properly watching. Conversations dipped into whispers between deliveries, and even the beer snakes in Bay 13 had crawled to a halt. The odd clap for a well-left delivery. Someone a few seats away pulled out a weather app and nudged their mate. There was an unspoken sense we were entering the final act of something, even though there was a lot of play left in the match.

Australia's innings was unravelling. One wicket, then another, then a long, tense patch before the next. It was like the game had slowed just enough for everyone to feel the weight of each ball. And then, sometime in the final hour, they were 9 wickets down with a 333-run lead. Funnily, India had ended Day 3 on 9 down, and now here we were again. Same situation. Different team. It wasn't a big moment, but it felt like a neat little full stop. Like the match had folded in on itself for a second, giving us this quiet, mirrored beat before whatever came next.

Since I didn't have any engagements that evening, I figured it was time to properly test Melbourne's food scene. Supernormal back on Day 2 had left a pretty strong impression, so expectations were high. I wandered into Chinatown and, within minutes, was surrounded by queues that looked more like people waiting for concert tickets than dinner. I skipped the madness and found a small Indonesian spot that had just the right mix of great smells and available seating. On the way out, I treated myself with one of those soft serves everyone seemed to be holding. It had been a full day, not in the noisy, social way some of the others had been, but in a way that still left me feeling like I'd squeezed every drop out of it.

Day 5

Most people watching a Test match on TV don't realise this, but Day 5 at an Australian Test comes with a bit of behind-the-scenes suspense. Unlike the first four days, Day 5 tickets aren't released in advance. That's because many matches wrap up within four days, so Cricket Australia waits until the end of Day 4 to decide whether to open the gates for the final day. If the match is still alive at stumps on Day 4, then and only then does the announcement come. Sometimes it flashes on the big screen at the ground. Other times, it just appears on the website later that evening.

And even then, it's not like you can just hop online and book your favourite seat. For Day 5, the tickets are either available at the booking counter in front of the stadium or online for those brief few hours between the two days' play. Plus, it's general admission only. No reserved seating, no assigned rows. You get in, and you find whatever spot you can. Which sounds easy enough until you remember this is the MCG and you're competing with thousands of other die-hard fans who all had the same idea. So, when I decided I was going, I wasn't going casually. I was going early. I was going prepared.

I knew exactly where I wanted to be. P20, Row A – ideally Seat 1 or 2, but I'd take anything in that stretch. I'd sat there the day before and couldn't stop thinking about the view. Elevated just enough to catch the angles, close enough to feel inside the match, and right near the camera well, which gave it this strangely official vibe. That night, I mapped the whole thing out in my head. Which gate opened earliest, which staircase would get me up fastest, where the lines might slow me down. I probably visualised it more times than I've prepared for any exam. But when a spot feels right, it's hard to ignore. And on this final day, I didn't just want to watch the cricket. I wanted to be right there, exactly where I felt it most.

I reached the ground by 8 am, much earlier than most but not early enough to avoid the inevitable queue. A long line had already formed outside the gates, with that familiar Melbourne Test morning buzz in the air. General admission meant everyone was out to grab the best possible seat they could find, and no one was taking that lightly. Among the early risers were the usual characters: die-hard fans strategising with their mates, groups from the suburbs settling in with breakfast and banter, and plenty of solo pilgrims like me who had mapped out their game-day seats in advance.

Of course, there were the usual suspects – someone standing in line alone, only for a large group to casually join them later, claiming a place they hadn't earned. Earlier in life, I might have just sighed and let it pass, but not now. When the latecomer group arrived, I told them politely but firmly that it wasn't fair to those who had actually queued. I asked them to head to the back instead. They looked a bit taken aback. I wasn't trying to pick a fight – I just wanted everyone to have a good day at the cricket, and that starts with respecting each other's time. It might seem like a small thing, but in moments like that, you realise how much the crowd's energy, and the way people treat each other, can make or break the whole experience.

When the gates finally opened, I moved like I had purpose. Not sprinting, but that fast, focused walk you do when every second counts and you don't want to draw attention. (To be fair, I do think I was being a bit over-dramatic at that point.) I knew exactly where to go. I didn't pause to check the signs. Up the ramp, past a couple of confused volunteers and straight into P20. And there it was, completely empty. Not a soul in sight. Just rows of untouched seats and the kind of soft morning light that makes everything feel a bit more cinematic than it probably deserved to be.

I didn't sit down straight away. Instead, I gave myself a little tour of the front row, like a homebuyer doing final inspections. One seat was too close to the stairwell, which meant a steady stream of people walking past all day. Another had a slightly awkward angle to the crease, which wasn't bad, but I wouldn't settle. Eventually, I landed on a seat tucked into the corner. Still front row, but angled just right to catch everything. Plus, it had a quick escape route to the aisle, in case I needed to grab a drink or just stand and stretch. I dropped my bag beside me and took a deep breath. This was it. This was my seat.

I settled in and watched the MCG slowly come alive. The seats around me began to fill, but not all at once – it was more like a quiet stream than a crowd surge. You could tell who came for the cricket and who came for the photos. The lower bays were already dotted with people angling for selfies and wide shots, especially right up near the boundary rope. But up in P20, it was a different kind of energy. No big flags, no chants, no standing up after every ball. Just people who showed up with their water bottles and sunhats, happy to sit through a slow session if it meant watching a good spell build.

Once play started, every now and then someone would whisper a guess about who'd take the next over, but mostly, we all just watched. And even though it was a Monday, the crowd was strong. That weird New Year's week energy was still hanging in the air filled with the vibes of holidays and a Test match still alive on Day 5. If you were in Melbourne and even remotely cricket-inclined, there really was no excuse not to be here.

...

I hadn't even properly settled into my seat when Australia's innings wrapped up. Three overs in, one loose shot, and that was that, all out. It felt like someone had hit fast forward. Suddenly, India was walking out with 334 runs to chase and a whole day to do it. No drama, no delay, just straight into the final act.

The session until tea wasn't great for India. A couple of early wickets had shifted the momentum, and by the time the players walked off for the break, it already felt like they'd need something special to stay in the game. I hadn't even noticed the change in my neighbour until I glanced to my right and saw someone in an IPL jersey settling in. We exchanged a quick nod, started chatting, and that's how I met Vignesh.

He was rocking a Chennai Super Kings jersey, which told me two things straight off the bat. One, the man backed his cricket. Two, there was no way this was going to be a boring session. He worked in tech too, so we briefly geeked out about our work in tech and AI, but what really struck me was his energy. He had this quiet, analytical way of watching the game. No unnecessary commentary, no overexcited reactions, just a thoughtful presence, like someone you'd find in the stands at Chepauk, part of that famously knowledgeable Chennai crowd. The types who clap for a good leave and spot a bowling change two overs before it happens. Sitting beside him felt like cricket with subtitles. He didn't talk much, but when he did, it always made me pause and go, 'Ah, good point'. Honestly, if you're going to spend hours watching a tense Test session with a stranger, Vignesh was exactly the kind of company you'd hope for.

Things didn't pick up much after the break either. The wickets kept tumbling, the target started to feel more like a deadline, and you could sense the buzz in the crowd shifting to nervous murmurs. By lunch, India was three down, and any hopes of a heroic chase were now hanging by the thinnest of threads. The only real thread, in fact, was Jaiswal. He was still out there, calm and composed, batting like he hadn't read the script everyone else was following. At that point, he didn't just look like our best chance – he looked like our only one.

During the break, I stepped out to get some food. That's when I wandered into this pocket of chaos just outside the stadium. Not fans this time, but media folks buzzing around with their cameras and mics, filming quick updates with the match at a crucial juncture. That's when I spotted Boria Majumdar. If you've followed Indian cricket even a little, you've probably seen his face on TV or his name on a book cover. On screen, he's all passion and intensity, but in that moment, he was relaxed, approachable and happily posed for a photo with me. I hung around for a minute, watching other Indian journalist crews sending match reports back home. Loud voices, dramatic takes, and I was taken right back to watching TV in India. India still had a technical chance, sure, but if you went by the energy around the cameras, we were already packing up to go home.

As the match wore on, it started feeling less like a chase and more like a slow bleed. Jaiswal was still out there, looking as unbothered as ever, steadily accumulating runs while the rest of the batting order seemed to be in a hurry to leave. The other end kept emptying out, one dismissal at a time, and the scoreboard wasn't helping anyone's nerves. People around me sighed, muttered under their breath, or just shook their heads in silence. Some had already started preparing themselves for the worst, others still clung to hope because Jaiswal was still there. But by the time the second tea break rolled around, even that hope was starting to feel stretched. The excitement had drained out of the crowd, and I found myself sitting back, not thinking about targets anymore, just hoping for a miracle. Not because it made sense, but because it's cricket, and sometimes that's all you've got left.

Maybe that's the thing about test cricket. Somewhere along the way, it stops being about technique or score lines or strategies. It becomes something else entirely. A stubborn kind of belief. A quiet kind of faith. The kind that makes you sit under a baking sun for five days just to see if the universe might tilt a little in your team's favour. It's irrational, sure, but it's also beautiful. Because every once in a while, when hope looks far away, cricket gives you that moment. That one delivery, that one innings, that one roar from the crowd that makes you believe again.

That miracle? Yeah, it didn't show up that day. Not even fashionably late. Once Jaiswal fell, with his controversial dismissal creating quite a stir in the crowd, it was like someone flicked off the last light switch. The air went out of the stadium and I could practically hear people groaning in six different languages. The rest of the batting line-up didn't exactly put up a fight either, and it felt as if they'd quietly packed up and left the building. A polite surrender.

And then, it was done. Not with a twist or a fight to the finish, but with a soft, inevitable thud. One last wicket, a few cheers from the Aussie sections, and just like that, the chase came to an end. No drama. No miracle. Just a slow walk back to the pavilion and the scoreboard frozen in place. Around me, people started gathering their belongings, stretching their legs after a long day of cricket. Some looked disappointed, some content, most just looked ready for dinner. I sat there for a bit longer, not really upset, just still. Five days of stories, strangers, sunburns and cricket in all its glory. It didn't end with glory – it did, of course, for Australia – but it ended with clarity. I came here for a match, but what I got was an experience. And sometimes, that's the real win.

I finally peeled myself away from the seat and started the shuffle out of the stadium, still thinking about Jaiswal's knock and how close, yet far, it all felt. Just outside, I spotted Angad Bedi and Neha Dhupia, two Bollywood celebrities, both looking like they'd rather be anywhere else. I asked for a selfie anyway. Angad agreed, begrudgingly. The photo is great if you ignore his face, and mine, honestly – two very different kinds of disappointment in one frame.

From there, I did what I always do with a mildly broken heart, or a happy heart - I got a good bowl of Laksa. It was hot, spicy, and just the thing to wash down a five-day rollercoaster. I wandered through Chinatown for a while, dodging the growing evening crowds and letting the buzz of the city take over. The match was done but my time in Melbourne wasn't. I still had New Year's Day to look forward to, and something else lined up soon after – something that would bring me right back to the heart of cricket, but in a way I hadn't experienced before.

Interlude

It was December 31st, the last day of 2024. I woke up without an alarm. For the first time in days, there was no rush to beat the queues at Gate 2, no WhatsApp group buzzing with ticket strategies or lunch break predictions. Even so, my eyes opened early, somewhere around 5.30 am. It felt like my body hadn't quite accepted that the match was over. Outside, it was 31 December – the last day of the year. Normally, a day like that would hum with anticipation, full of noise and countdown energy. But Melbourne felt strangely still.

I stepped out into a city that looked nothing like the one I'd been living in for the past week. The footpaths were empty, cafe chairs still stacked from the night before. The only sound was the low whirr of a tram sliding by without any passengers. Even the birds seemed to be pacing themselves. Morning light slipped between buildings, touching the cobblestones with a soft, golden glow. When I passed the parliament building, I could hear my own footsteps bounce off its stone walls. For a moment, I wondered if this stillness was just the calm before the fireworks later that night. Maybe people were resting in anticipation, saving their energy. Or maybe I was only now realising how loud the last five days had really been. After all that noise, applause and crowd chants, this kind of quiet felt strange. But I welcomed it. It felt like the city was catching its breath, and I was doing the same.

Even my footsteps felt too loud. I wandered without a plan, half expecting the city to wake up around me. But it didn't. And somewhere along the way, the silence started to follow me inwards. For five days, my thoughts had been moving to someone else's rhythm – score updates, seat plans, the buzz of Bay 13. Every morning had been built around a shared sense of anticipation. But now that the urgency had slipped away, something slower began to surface in its place. My mind drifted back to the match, not because I wanted to analyse it, but because it refused to leave me alone.

The match kept coming back to me in pieces – Konstas's legendary innings, Bumrah's five-wicket haul, the late afternoons pulsing with tension. It didn't feel like a game I had just watched. It felt like something I had lived.

There are some things you can simply only see at the ground, like the way a bowler walks back to his mark after a tough over, the way fielders reposition themselves without direction, or the collective hum of focus between deliveries. In the stadium, those moments are sharp. You feel the rhythm of effort, the weight of decision-making. You see commitment. Not just in the wickets taken, but in the balls that are fought over and lost. Especially in the ones that are lost. Those are the deliveries that stay with you. The ones where the bowler tries something and it doesn't work, but he still jogs back to his mark with the same resolve. The ones where the batter plays and misses, but then digs in even harder. From a seat in the stands, you learn to admire the struggle itself, not just the sixes and wickets, but the unseen war for control.

That's what stood out most to me about Australia. Not just their performance but the persistence underneath it. Pat Cummins, especially, whether batting, fielding or bowling, kept showing up, ball after ball, as if nothing else existed. Even when the play wasn't going their way, there was never a dip in intensity. And it wasn't just him. A quiet discipline ran through the whole team, a kind of collective refusal to switch off.

In contrast, India had its flashes. Jaiswal brought elegance, Nitish Kumar Reddy showed real defiance, and Bumrah was thundering like ever. But I didn't feel the same relentlessness. There were moments of brilliance, yes, but they didn't stack up into something sustained. I saw greatness in stretches, but not grit over time. Or rather, I saw grit in isolated pockets, not as a system. I know it's a hard thing to admit, but it felt like Australia was simply more invested in every ball. More ready to do the boring stuff. More willing to earn their victories one over at a time.

And maybe that's why the match felt so full. I wasn't just watching cricket. I was watching people push themselves, fall short, and dig deeper. It brought back memories of the first match I ever saw in Bijapur back in 1995 in a small stand and a much simpler time. In both matches, however, the feeling was the same. That mix of awe and hunger, of knowing you're lucky to be there. This wasn't just a Test match. It was the kind of cricket that reminds you why you fell in love with the game in the first place.

At some point, I opened Google Maps just to see what was nearby. I wasn't looking for anything in particular, just scanning the area out of habit. That's when I noticed a marker for a war memorial a short walk away. I didn't know what it was exactly, but it seemed close enough and open so I turned in that direction. A few minutes later, I found myself at the foot of the Shrine of Remembrance. The path leading up to it was long and straight, flanked by open lawns and trimmed trees, with the building sitting high above the city like it had been waiting. I didn't rush. There was a stillness to it, the kind that made you slow down without realising. The stone steps were wide and solemn, and the structure ahead looked less like a monument and more like a statement. I didn't know much about its history at that point, only that it honoured Australians who had served in war. But something about the way it sat there, unbothered by time or noise, made me pause.

I almost always take guided tours. It's just easier. You get to hear the bits you'd otherwise miss, and someone else does the job of deciding where to look. This one was led by a senior woman, friendly in that specific way tour guides are when they've said the same lines a hundred times but still mean them. She pointed out this shaft of light built into the shrine's roof where, she said, on 11 November at exactly 11 am, the light passes through and lands perfectly on a stone that says, 'Greater love hath no man.' I don't know why that detail stuck with me, but it did. It was quiet, precise, and strangely moving.

Then there was the view from the top, where you can spot the face of an Aboriginal man, William Barak, staring back from a skyscraper in the distance. The symbolism wasn't lost on anyone, but nobody really said anything. We just stood there, facing a city that's always building forward, while standing inside a place built to remember. At one point, the guide mentioned that Rudyard Kipling had written the original inscription for the shrine, but they made him rewrite it. I couldn't help but smile at that. Even Kipling got edits. I don't have any personal military connection, but I did go to a military school, so maybe that explains why this place didn't feel distant. It wasn't emotional in the usual way. It just felt like something worth standing still for.

Leaving the memorial, I found myself back near the Yarra, a part of the city that had quietly threaded itself through the week. It always seems to be just around the corner. When a crossing came, I took it, and on the bridge I heard 'Yaara O Yaara', an Indian song playing softly from someone's phone. It's the kind of song you'd expect at weddings or long road trips back home, not echoing over a Melbourne river. But the moment I heard it, I knew exactly what had happened. The river was called Yarra, the song was 'Yaara', and the fun of that little overlap hadn't been lost on the group of Indian tourists nearby. They had clearly decided it was too good a coincidence to pass up. A few steps later, another thought landed. In Hindi, *yaar* means mate, and in Australia, there's probably no word more sacred. Somehow, this one river managed to carry both meanings.

About half an hour later I found myself at the Royal Botanic Gardens. I'd ended up at the one in Brisbane at the start of this trip, so maybe this was turning into a bit of a pattern. Big city, long walk, quiet green space in the middle. I didn't linger. Just walked through, let it reset the day a little, and kept moving along the river when I saw her. She was sitting on a low stool by the edge of the path on the riverbank, completely absorbed in her painting. No music, no signboard. Just a canvas, a palette, and the view in front of her with trees, water and the soft outline of buildings tucked in behind them.

I didn't say anything right away. I just stood there for a bit, watching her paint. There was something so self-contained about the whole scene. She wasn't performing for anyone. She wasn't trying to sell anything. It was just something she clearly loved doing. I could feel it in the way she stayed completely focused, unbothered by people walking past or the noise drifting over from the other side of the river. The whole scene had a quiet kind of rhythm to it – the sound of the water, the brush moving across the canvas, the steady presence of someone doing something they clearly cared about. I didn't want to interrupt, so I waited a little, just letting the moment settle.

Eventually, I stepped a little closer and asked if she was selling her work. She looked up and smiled, but didn't seem to follow what I was saying. So we both pulled out our phones and started typing into Google Translate. I told her I really liked what she was working on, and if she was open to it, I'd love to buy it once it was finished. She read it, paused, then smiled again and nodded. She typed back that it would take about forty-five minutes. I said I'd come back. When I did, she handed it to me gently. The paint was still a little wet at the edges and it looked just like what I'd seen earlier, but seeing it on canvas gave it a kind of stillness I hadn't noticed at the time. I asked how much, but she didn't name a price. Just smiled, like it was up to me. I offered something that felt fair, and she nodded. I rolled it up and tucked it away carefully. It's still at home now, tucked away. I haven't framed it yet. Maybe I just like having a few things that stay unfinished, like they still belong to the moment they came from.

...

The day felt sluggish, like it had struggled to get out of bed. Now it started to slow down even more, and so had I. I didn't feel like heading back to the hotel, but I wasn't exactly in the mood to keep walking either, so I did the most sensible thing I could think of: bought a ticket for a movie. What better way to pass a few hours than sitting in a dark room and turning my brain off?

By the time I stepped out, it was 9 pm and the tempo had well and truly changed: the city was packed with people excited for the midnight fireworks. I didn't have a plan. I just followed the crowd until I ended up near Federation Square, which wasn't too packed. And by not too packed, I mean at least I wasn't getting squished to death. People were laying out mats, opening chip packets, taking blurry photos. I didn't talk to anyone, just sat there for a while. It was one of those moments where the city feels oddly unified with thousands of people doing absolutely nothing, just waiting for something loud and sparkly to tell them the year's over.

The wait dragged a little, but no one really seemed to mind. People kept checking their phones, laughing at nothing, passing around snacks. And then, without much warning, the fireworks began. The first few lit up the sky and a wave of cheering rippled through the crowd. I looked up and let it all happen. Bright colours, loud bangs, people yelling 'Happy New Year!' in unison. I didn't end up filming anything; not because I was trying to be in the moment or anything noble like that. I just forgot. The whole thing wrapped up pretty fast. Decent fireworks, solid crowd and a nice excuse to smile at strangers. Sometimes, that's all you need.

...

Melbourne had given me more than I had expected. But before I left, I wanted to see what lay behind the gates I'd only ever entered as a fan. No crowd this time. No roar, no music, no sea of blue and gold. Just a slow walk toward the MCG on a bright January morning, with nothing but time on my hands and a bit of curiosity still left to burn.

By 9 am I was walking back to the stadium again. Same footpath, same route, but the energy was completely different. No streams of people, no merchandise stalls spilling onto the pavement, no one chanting players' names into the morning air. Just me, a coffee in hand and the soft buzz of a city returning to normal. I wasn't going back for a match. I was going to see the bones of the place, the underlayers of the ground where I'd just spent five days completely immersed. I was going in for a guided tour of the Melbourne Cricket Ground. Simple enough on paper, but to me, it felt like peeling back the surface of something I thought I knew.

Walking through the inside of the MCG felt a bit surreal. Not quite like a museum, not exactly like a temple, but somewhere in that middle space where you instinctively lower your voice without being told. There were only about a dozen of us on the tour and everyone kept pretty quiet. Just footsteps and the occasional comment from the guide. I found myself looking up at the empty stands, thinking about how they were completely packed, loud and alive just a couple of days ago. Now, here I was, retracing it all but from the other side. It almost felt like stepping back into a memory, except this time, the memory was one of mine. The dressing rooms were smaller than I expected. Nothing fancy – just benches, hooks, a couple of screens and a quiet stillness in the air, like the room hadn't quite exhaled yet.

Outside, there was a board listing all the support staff for both teams. The difference was hard to miss; the Indian list stretched far longer than Australia's – more than two times the length. Sure, they were the visiting side, and maybe that's normal, but it made me pause. I found myself wondering whether all that backup came at a cost. Did having so many layers around the players create too much distance from the game itself? Too much comfort? I didn't dwell on it, but the thought lingered as we moved on.

Back inside, I kept imagining Bumrah sitting here. Jadeja lacing up. Khawaja humming something under his breath. Watching them from the stands, they felt untouchable. But here, it was easier to picture the nerves, the silence before the storm, and the room being filled with just a bunch of people trying to steady themselves before stepping into chaos.

We turned a corner and stepped into the museum section of the stadium. Right in front of me was a display already set up for the Test I'd just watched – a summary of the match and the actual match ball, mounted neatly behind glass. I remember just standing there for a second, taking it in. It felt strange that the game had only just ended, and here it was already part of the MCG's official history. Part of me was quietly thrilled. I'd been there; seen it all unfold. But another part of me couldn't help but feel how quickly the game moved on. That something so fresh in my memory had already become a museum piece.

I think I expected the match to linger a little longer, at least in the present tense. To still belong to the fans, to the debates on group chats, to the players themselves before it got wrapped up and archived. But the MCG had already filed it away, slotted it into a timeline that would outlast us all. And that did something to me. It made the whole experience feel bigger than the five days I spent watching it. Like I'd briefly stepped into something that would carry on long after I'd gone back to work, back to life. I hadn't just seen a game. I'd watched a little slice of history take shape and then watched it quietly move on.

Near the end of the tour we passed the Shane Warne statue. I'd seen it before from the outside with him in that classic mid-delivery pose, but seeing it now, after walking through the insides of the stadium, felt different. It had a quiet weight to it. I looked back one last time at the ground itself, standing tall and still in the summer light, and weirdly, the first thought in my mind was that the Gabba needed a rebuild. That ground had its own charm, no doubt, but it was tucked away awkwardly and everything around it made you feel like you were sneaking in cricket between errands. The parking was a hassle, the roads always felt tense, and stepping out after a great day at the game meant being dumped straight into peak-hour chaos. At the Gabba, you had to fight for the right to enjoy cricket. It felt transactional, like a duel you won for the privilege of watching the game. The MCG, though, breathed differently. There was space around it. Parks, trees, trams gliding by. The stadium wasn't just a venue; it was part of the city's rhythm. Being there didn't feel like a battle. It felt like a slow dance, a kind of romance between the ground and the people who came to it. It invited you in and gave you room to feel something. Walking away from it felt like leaving a cathedral – not just of sport, but of memory.

    I didn't stay much longer after that. I picked up my bag, caught an Uber and headed to the airport. It felt quiet again, but a different kind of quiet; the kind that comes after something has ended well. On the flight back to Sydney, I ended up in the front row and couldn't help but laugh a little at the symmetry. After five days of front-row seats at the MCG, of feeling close to every moment, it somehow made sense to finish the trip this way too. I leaned back, looked out the window as the city slipped away beneath the clouds, and let it all settle. Melbourne had given me a summer to remember. And now it was time to go home for the last hurrah.

CHAPTER 4

NEW YEAR'S TEST/PINK TEST, SYDNEY

Days 0 and 1

I've never been good at packing, or planning my time well when it comes to packing for trips. For someone who prides himself on colour-coded Google calendar entries and spreadsheet grocery lists, there's something about stuffing a suitcase that makes me irrationally confident until it's far too late. Which is how I found myself, on 2 January, standing in my living room with three open bags, a half-zipped duffel and no idea where my power bank was. My flight to India was on 8 January, which was just one day after the Sydney Test wrapped up, and it was starting in less than twenty-four hours. I had somehow left everything till now.

I don't know if it was the festive lull after New Year's, or the post-Melbourne daze still swirling in my head, but the realisation hit like a short ball I never saw coming. This wasn't just a regular trip back home. This time, I was planning to stay for a while. A good month, in fact. Back to my hometown in Karnataka to see family, to catch up with people I'd kept meaning to visit. Which meant not just packing clothes, but packing with purpose – gifts, clothes, souvenirs I spent wayyy too much money on at the MCG, all the good stuff. I panicked a little. Then I panicked a lot. And then, in true form, I threw whatever I could find into the bags, convinced I'd sort it out somehow. Little did I know then that I'd have plenty of time to repack everything.

But, even as I was frantically shoving things into suitcases, my mind kept drifting to the match. This one felt different. Not because of the venue, though. The Sydney Cricket Ground (SCG) wasn't some unfamiliar pilgrimage. I'd been there more times than I could count. In fact, it's kind of a family tradition at this point to take the kids to watch WBBL (Women's Big Bash League) matches and at least one day of the Pink Test every year. So, I knew this ground. I knew where the good coffee was, where the shade started creeping by the second session, and which section's crowd always went too hard too early. But somehow, this didn't feel routine. It felt big.

Part of it was the stakes. After four gripping Tests, Australia was on the cusp of winning the series, leading at 2–1. If India won, the series tied and the Border–Gavaskar Trophy stayed with them, as it had for the last eight years. But if Australia won, or even managed to draw? They'd take the cup back. That possibility had everyone on edge. And despite the chaos around me, I couldn't help but feel the buzz of it too.

And then, of course, there was the familiar question I never quite knew how to answer: who was I even supporting? Born in India, citizen of Australia. Proud of my Indian heritage and equally proud of the Australian values. I'd cheered for Kohli's centuries and Cummins's yorkers with equal joy. So I did what I always do – I leaned into the game. I wasn't there to take sides. I just wanted to see how it all played out.

The next day, I woke up early. Though I always wake up around the same time, this morning felt less like discipline and more like pre-match electricity. It was the kind of early where you don't even need an alarm because your brain has already sprinted ahead, mentally packing sunscreen, triple-checking ticket PDFs, and wondering whether the security staff will let you bring in homemade sandwiches (they do).

Luckily, one part of the plan had been sorted well in advance: parking. Now, this is where I must pause and offer a public service announcement to all future Sydney cricket enthusiasts, especially the ones who think it's a good idea to just find a spot on the day of the match or brave the 40-kilometre public transport haul from the outer suburbs.

Don't do that. Book your parking at the QVB with Wilson Parking.

Book it early. Like, four days early. You'll lock in a spot right in the middle of the city for what is basically loose change compared to same-day rates. Plus, you're walking distance from an actual toilet and decent coffee. Then, hop on the light rail and enjoy the glorious fifteen-minute tram ride to Moore Park with no transfers, no platform guessing and no train-station drama. It's the Test match equivalent of finding a hundred-dollar note in your old jeans. Thank me later.

By the time I'd parked, trammed and emerged into the growing pink tide outside the SCG, I felt oddly calm. Everything had worked. My bag was light, my timing was perfect and I still had sunscreen in my hand. I pumped my chest and walked like a man with a plan. And this plan was a little more than just watching the match, I was attending a breakfast hosted by the Primary Club of Australia.

Now, I hadn't heard of the Primary Club of Australia until I got the invite, and discovering them felt like one of those serendipitous gifts this summer kept offering. Their mission is beautifully simple: every time a professional cricketer gets out for a duck, members donate to support athletes with disabilities. That's it. It's the kind of idea that slips under the radar, but once you hear it, you can't stop thinking about how right it feels. Humble, purposeful, and very cricket.

The breakfast itself was held on the morning of Day 1 of the Sydney Test, and it's a bit of a tradition at the SCG. Irfan Malik, who we met earlier, had been hearing about my cricket travels and kindly offered me an invite. AIBC was one of the partners for the event. It was a wonderful New Year's gift and I was very excited to attend the breakfast event.

Inside, it was a mix of nostalgia and networking. There were white tablecloths, polite applause and a menu that could have been lifted straight from a five-star hotel buffet. But the heart of the morning was a panel discussion titled State of the Game, featuring Mark Taylor, Ed Cowan and Cricinfo editor Andrew McGlashan. It wasn't just small talk or highlight reels, they offered frank insights on where the game stood, what was working, and what needed fixing. Taylor brought his statesman-like calm, Cowan was thoughtful and reflective, and McGlashan added the sharp edge of someone who watches the sport with both love and scrutiny. While there was a certain heft and seriousness to the conversation, it was also very refreshing and natural. You could see that everyone on the panel and in the room in general was engaged and excited about the game ahead.

Somewhere between the eggs Benedict and the raffle for Pat Cummins's signed bat, I found myself genuinely moved by what the Primary Club was doing. It was a reminder that cricket isn't only about bat and ball. It's about connection and causes that quietly build momentum in the background while the spotlight stays on the field. I signed up as a member right at the event thanks to the QR codes conveniently placed at every table. Who would've thought QR codes, a mechanism invented in Japan for labelling auto parts, would become such a ubiquitous part of our lives!

It turned out my neighbour at the table was Mohit Kumar, a local councillor I'd seen at other events. We had a brief chat about two things we had in common: cricket and Blacktown (our local council), and then I made my way to the book sales counter. There they were: signed copies of Pat Cummins's autobiography. The book had been on my reading list for a while and these were of course signed copies! I asked how many they'd let one person buy because I didn't want to be that guy sweeping the whole pile. They had a small limit per guest, which made sense. I picked up the maximum allowed. Some for me, some for a few people back in India who'd know exactly why this mattered. Because if there's one thing I've learned, it's that cricket books make excellent surprise gifts, especially when they're signed. And even more so when you can hand one over with a casual, 'Oh, it's nothing. Just something I picked up at breakfast with Mark Taylor.'

...

Once the speeches wound down and people started drifting toward the coffee tables, I slipped out and began the short five-minute walk to the SCG. Blazer still on, sunscreen packed, mildly sweating but I could feel the buzz kicking in. Even before I reached the gate, the pink had already taken over. Shirts, hats, pink Marios, the SCG turns fully technicolour for the Pink Test, and Sydney never does it halfway. I've walked into this ground more times than I can count, but there's something about this match that always hits differently.

If you're reading this and wondering why everything suddenly turned pink – no, you didn't skip a page, and I haven't wandered into a flamingo exhibition by mistake. The first Sydney Test of the year is also known as the Pink Test, a tradition started by the McGrath Foundation to raise funds for breast cancer support. Technically, only Day 3 is the official Pink Day, but Sydney's never been great at doing things quietly so the colour spills out early, and no one seems to mind. That's the thing about cricket. It's not just a sport, it's a culture where people show up, show out, and somehow turn something as serious as cancer into a day of joy, noise and solidarity. Everyone's wearing their own shade of pink, but somehow, it all fits together.

I was doing my part too – pink cap, pink blazer, fully committed. Pink's not exactly my staple, but here, on this day, it felt completely natural. Like the colour belonged, and so did I, just by wearing it. That's the magic of the Pink Test.

Outside the stadium, the lines felt less like a queue and more like a festival. A full-blown procession had formed near the forecourt. Led, of course, by the Indian community. Women in bright pink saris, some embroidered with sequins that caught the morning light, were handing out ribbons and selfies in equal measure. A couple of kids were beating out rhythms on small *dhols* while their parents stood nearby, proudly pink and slightly sun-blocked. It wasn't loud in a chaotic way, more of a we've-done-this-before way. Familiar, celebratory and completely at home in front of the SCG.

I soaked it in, scanned my ticket, and made my way to my seat. The sun was already sharp, the energy sharper, and in a few minutes, the cricket would begin.

The first hour was a blur, and not the good kind. India was two down by the eighth over, and it felt like no one had told the top order that the match had actually started. I remember glancing at the scoreboard, seeing the second wicket fall and instinctively reaching for my water bottle like hydration might fix what was clearly spiraling on the field. And then Kohli, I swear, nearly joined them. A thick edge, nowhere near convincing, and somehow, by a stroke of luck, the ball touched the ground for a nanosecond before being caught. As the third umpire reviewed the catch, I didn't breathe. Just sat there, waiting to see if he would walk. He didn't. Pure luck. But enough to make me sit up and realise that this wasn't going to be one of those drift-in-and-enjoy-the-sun kind of Tests.

By lunch, things weren't much better. We were three down and still stuck in the double digits. The crowd had quietened. Not dramatically, but enough that you could tell people were checking the score more often than they were checking their phones. And with the Border–Gavaskar Trophy on the line, that silence carried a bit of weight. If India lost this, the trophy went back to Australia. After eight years of holding onto it, the idea of letting it go wasn't exactly welcome. Someone needed to shift the gears soon.

I took the chance to stretch my legs and grab something to eat, ending up with two *vada pavs* (Indian street-style burgers). I had one on the spot, realising it was not actually bad – better than expected, considering the setting. I took my time walking back, partly to let the food settle and partly because I wasn't in a hurry to see another wicket. As I walked back into the bay, vada pav in hand, I kept hearing the crowd yell, 'Chug! Chug! Chug! Chug!' At first, I was thoroughly confused. I looked down at the *vada pav*; surely they weren't expecting me to chug this thing? But then I turned around and saw the real target: a guy just behind me, carrying four plastic cups of beer, trying to make his way up the stairs without spilling too much or being publicly shamed.

The rule (unwritten, of course) was that if you showed up with more than one beer, you had to chug at least one before you were allowed to pass. It wasn't enforced by anyone official, but the bay wouldn't let you go without trying. If you managed to get it down in time and hold your footing, they cheered you like you'd just taken a blinder at first slip. If you didn't, no matter if you hesitated, sipped or spilled, you were met with theatrical boos and groans. It was childish, ridiculous and absolutely brilliant. I took my seat and watched the whole thing unfold like a mini sport within the sport. At one point, I genuinely forgot the cricket was back on. Until another wicket fell quicker than anyone expected it to.

The rest of the day didn't exactly slow down. India was bowled out for 185, and honestly, it felt like we barely blinked between wickets. One moment Kohli was surviving by luck, the next we were into the tail and wondering if lunch had been the high point of the innings. The crowd around me had long stopped pretending it wasn't a collapse; we all knew what we were watching. It wasn't just the scoreline. It was the way it happened – loose shots, unlucky nicks, not enough fight. It felt like a team stuck between holding on and hoping for something to happen. And on days like that, cricket doesn't wait.

Australia came in late in the day, and for a while it looked like they'd just cruise till stumps. Sam Konstas, fresh off his Melbourne heroics, was at it again, needling Bumrah while at the non-striker's end. There was something undeniably refreshing about an eighteen year old standing up to the world's best fast bowler without blinking. And yet, a small part of me didn't love it. Not because he wasn't good enough, clearly, he was, but because it felt like poking a sleeping lion. You don't do that. Not to Bumrah.

And, right on cue, the lion roared.

On the very next ball, Usman Khawaja edged one to KL Rahul at slip. The day hadn't belonged to India, not by a long shot, but that single moment gave us something to cheer for. It didn't change the match, but it changed the mood. And sometimes, that's more than enough.

...

The worst part about attending a match in your own city is that you have to go back to your own home at the end of the day. There's no hotel room waiting for you. No quick walk across the street. No dinner plan that someone else arranged. Just an hour-and-a-half commute that ends with you kicking off your shoes in silence.

In Brisbane, I was staying less than ten minutes from the ground. In Melbourne, I could see the stadium from where I slept. But here, in Sydney, my own city, I had to drag myself back to North-West Sydney, through the whole post-match migration of light rail, parking garage and freeway. The novelty had worn off. Reality had returned.

But no, I wasn't done yet. I had one more stop – a fundraiser hosted by IIMPACT, an NGO that funds the education of girl children in rural India. Now, if you're thinking, what's that got to do with watching cricket? Fair question. I probably would've skipped it too ... if the main speaker wasn't Harsha Bhogle. And let's be honest, if you've watched even ten minutes of cricket in your life, you know who Harsha is. Everyone does. So you understand why I had to go. The match was done, my body wanted a shower and bed, but the blazer stayed on. Harsha was speaking. I was going.

The fundraiser was being held at the same hotel where the Indian cricket team was staying, which made the whole thing a bit more surreal. As I walked up, the team bus pulled in, and suddenly the entrance turned into a mini security fortress. I tried to enter but the guards weren't convinced.

'Guest list?' they asked.

'IIMPACT event,' I replied, pointing somewhere vaguely inside. While they sorted it out, I found myself standing next to Nitish Kumar Reddy, who was gracious enough to wait it out with me while I awkwardly explained that I was here for an NGO event, not a team meeting. Eventually, they directed me to a side entrance, but I'm choosing to remember it as walking in alongside the Indian team.

By the time I found the ballroom, I was properly spent. The match had taken its toll and my blazer felt heavier than it had all day. But the moment I walked in, the mood shifted. Now the vibe was that of round tables, soft lights and that unmistakable buzz of a well-organised fundraiser. This wasn't a cricket crowd anymore; it was a room full of people who cared about something bigger. Girl-child literacy through IIMPACT. And honestly, that made the whole evening feel worth the detour.

The highlight, of course, was Harsha Bhogle. He was introduced with much warmth and admiration, and the emcee's bio readout made half the room chuckle. It was that perfectly over-the-top kind of intro reserved for people you've grown up listening to. The interview itself was more structured than free flowing – the kind of format where the next question always feels slightly predictable – but the interviewer, Pawan Luthra of the Indian Link Media Group, carried it with his charm and wit. As expected, Harsha also responded with grace, generosity and the kind of polish you'd expect from someone who can make rain delays sound poetic. I would've loved to see a bit more of his wit let loose, but still, seeing him in person was the quiet thrill.

After the panel, people started hovering the way they do when someone vaguely famous is in the room but no one wants to be the first to ask for a photo. I waited, half-hoping the crowd would thin out. Eventually, I walked up, said hello, and thanked Harsha for the talk. He smiled – warm, generous, switched on – even though it was past 10 pm and he apparently had to get to the Eastern Suburbs before midnight, which made his energy seem even more impressive.

I mentioned the Dads and Daughters Cricket program and how I was keen to take it to India, getting some people from the cricketing fraternity into AIYD, and said I'd love to keep him in the loop for a few things. He nodded, told me his email. I typed it in right away so I wouldn't forget it, though I had a feeling it was one of those throwaway email addresses. And honestly, fair enough. Who's expecting Harsha Bhogle to hand out his personal email to every well-meaning stranger in a blazer? I wrote to him anyway. Didn't hear back. Maybe I'll get through with this book instead!

An hour later, I was driving home in silence. No music, no post-match shows. Just the hum of the freeway and the last image of Khawaja walking off at the end of the innings. I didn't need a summary. I'd lived the day.

Days 2 and 3

Day 2 was strange. Not in a bad way. Just not what you expect from a Test match. Usually, this is the day the play settles, like the middle overs of a five-day story. But this match had other plans.

Australia was bowled out in 51 overs. That's not a typo. Fifty-one. They made 180 and just … left. For a moment I wondered if I'd missed something, like maybe I'd tuned into the highlights by mistake. Test cricket doesn't usually move like that. But nope, India came swinging with the same energy too. Not just aggressive, just a bit impatient. They were playing strokes you'd usually reserve for a Sunday one-dayer. I thought it was just a phase, but then Rishabh Pant arrived and confirmed it: this was no longer a Test match. This was something else. The man batted like he was late for dinner. Everything flew off the bat – pulls, flicks, straight drives that didn't even bother looking elegant. It was all happening so fast, I was half expecting a strategic timeout.

I remember thinking, *If this keeps up, we might need Gavaskar on the mic just to yell 'Stupid, stupid, stupid' at every Indian dismissal.* The match was spiralling so fast, it felt like even the commentary needed a warning label.

That's not to say I wasn't loving it. I was, but I was also ... unsure. I like a bit of chaos in my cricket. I like unpredictability. But I also like the slow turns of a long game with momentum shifts, late-day quiet spells, the kind of tension you can sit with. This didn't have that. It was thrilling, but also kind of dizzying. And on top of that, I was juggling real life – applying for my Indian e-visa, checking emails, and realising I still hadn't figured out how I was going to properly pack everything in time. My flight was just one day after the Test was supposed to end. At this rate, though, with the way wickets were falling, there was a chance it wouldn't go five days at all. I didn't think too much of it at the time, but somewhere in the back of my mind, a quiet thought was forming: if this keeps up, I might just have time to breathe.

And time I did have. Because the next day, the match ended. Just like that. Three days. Done. What was supposed to be a five-day contest collapsed into a sprint finish. I walked into the ground expecting to settle in. Maybe we'd dig in and stretch things out. Maybe we'd fight for time, force a draw and protect the trophy. But by the first drinks break, I could feel the match slipping. The wickets weren't just falling; they were falling fast. Crisp, efficient, one after the other. Australia didn't even have to do anything extraordinary. India just kept losing shape.

I'd turned up in pink. A T-shirt from the Dads and Daughters program and, in a last-minute burst of commitment to the theme, I even bought a pink baseball cap outside the stadium. To top it off, and for reasons I still can't quite justify, I threw on a blazer. Not a pink blazer. Just a blazer. Don't ask me why. Maybe I just wanted to feel like I was still part of a proper five-day Test match. Whatever it was, the result was an outfit that looked like I'd forgotten to finish getting dressed, but at the time, it felt like the right call. Like I was showing up for something important, even if the match had other plans.

What made the downfall worse – or maybe just harder to watch – was that the approach hadn't changed. India had started batting like this the day before – taking risks, going after shots, playing like it was a limited-overs game. And fine, maybe that's the new template. Maybe that's just how this team plays. But now, on Day 3, with the series and the trophy on the line, they still weren't slowing down. We were batting like we needed to win, when all we really needed was to survive. The more I watched, the less I understood. If we got bowled out early, Australia would have two and a half days (two and a half!) to chase whatever total we left behind. And without Bumrah, who wasn't bowling due to injury, we were already a bowler short. It felt like we were setting up a race, but we were the ones handing out the stopwatch. A truly confusing moment for me that I still can't figure out.

India was bowled out for 164. Between both innings, we barely scraped together 350 runs. And just like that, the match tipped. With two and a half days left, Australia needed only 162 runs to win. Technically, there was still a chance. After all, they'd collapsed for 180 in the first innings too. So, if India bowled like their lives depended on it, if every fielder stayed sharp, and if we got a couple of early wickets, it could get interesting.

But, let's be honest. That kind of all-in intensity is hard to summon when you're short one of your best bowlers (and Australia knew it). More than that, they had two and a half bloody days to get there. No pressure. No scoreboard ticking. They didn't even have to play well. All they had to do was survive and the runs would come as a side effect. At that point, it stopped being a contest and turned into a countdown.

The rest played out exactly the way you'd expect it to. Australia won a few overs after lunch, taking the trophy after eight long years.

...

Fifteen minutes later, I was still sitting in my seat. Reminiscing. Just like that, it was over. The match, the series, the stadium buzz, all done in three days. No final-session cliffhanger. No fifth-day drama. Just an afternoon presentation, a polite exit and a strangely quiet walk back to the light rail. And it hit me, gently but firmly, that this was it – the end of My Summer of Cricket. I wasn't flying to Brisbane next week. I wasn't checking weather reports or plotting parking hacks or scouring for better seats online. There were no more mornings to wake up wondering which XI would show up. The rhythm I'd been living in, of play, pause, travel, repeat, had come to a full stop.

I'd met old friends, cousins, CEOs, diplomats, school alumni and strangers who felt like friends for the length of a match. I'd cheered from corporate glass and sweated it out in Row A. I'd watched collapses and comebacks, argued field placements with seat neighbours, stood for the anthems, waited out the clouds, and leaned into every moment that felt bigger than cricket.

I wasn't sad, exactly. Just still. And not quite ready to go home.

I was brought back to the present with my phone buzzing with a message. 'I'm near the merchandise store outside Gate E,' the message said. It was from Tejasvi Mohanram, with whom I'd been exchanging messages on Twitter for the last few days, and was planning to meet after the match.

While I started excitedly looking for him, I also let out a smile thinking about the sheer number of threads we had in common. It was the kind of smile that comes through naturally and effortlessly even though you are tired, brain working overtime analysing what could have been about the match and it's still sinking in that you've watched Virat Kohli play his last Test match in Australia.

Speaking of common threads, Tejasvi is a relative and also happens to be from the tech and entrepreneurship world. But most importantly, he was a senior at Sainik School in Bijapur. Although we didn't overlap at school, the connection to the institution is so strong that even the loosest thread of familiarity is enough to bind alumni together. I had flashbacks of waking up for 5 am drills every morning, always keeping your bed neat and tidy for any surprise inspections, learning how to march in parades with utmost precision and, of course, making sure to sing the national anthem in exactly fifty-two seconds! You held your seniors in high respect (or rather, were in fear of them), lowered your gaze when speaking with them, and called them sir.

Although, with Tejasvi, it was more a meeting with a fellow cricket and sport lover than with a senior from Sainik School. He'd made an impromptu plan to travel to Australia for the Border–Gavaskar Trophy, and I came across his plans when I saw him message a common connection on Twitter. Ah, it's crazy how it all comes together!

We caught up at a pub in Surry Hills; two Sainik School boys in Sydney, talking about winters in Bijapur, school parades, the pomegranate orchard on campus, scratchy uniforms, early morning assemblies and that particular brand of institutional toughness that only makes sense in hindsight. What surprised me wasn't how much we remembered, but how quickly we laughed about it. It was the kind of laughter that carries no agenda, just two people connecting over a time and place that shaped us in ways we're still decoding. The discussions simply carried on effortlessly and we ended up touching upon a huge range of topics – from getting kids into sport to world politics and, of course, the most important one, the future of Indian cricket!

Tejasvi's brother Yashasvi, joined us briefly too. Fun fact: he also went to Sainik School! In fact, Yashasvi and I had a one-year overlap at Sainik School. He was a final-year student (Year 12) when I'd just joined in Year 6. That six-year gap doesn't seem so big now, but it was so wide back then it might as well have been a different universe. I remember being in awe of Year 12s, and he, as I recalled, was one of the kind ones. He's still very much the kind and friendly person I remember him at school. He's now a partner at a law firm, sharp as ever, and just as easy to talk to.

Somewhere between the pints, the photos and the what-are-you-up-to-nows, it hit me: this was exactly thirty years since my first cricket match in Bijapur, in December 1994.

I still remember that day. It was a cold winter afternoon in Bijapur, or at least as cold as it gets in my part of India. The kind where you might finally get to wear full sleeves without regretting it by noon. My parents had brought me there to inquire about admissions at Sainik School but fate, or perhaps scheduling luck, had something extra in store: a Ranji One-Day match between Karnataka and Hyderabad at the Dr Ambedkar Stadium. I hadn't known it was on. I was just a kid tagging along for school admissions. But when we reached the stadium there were cricketers in whites, loudspeakers, scoreboards and a proper crowd. My day was no longer about school forms.

Back then, we didn't have a TV at home. My connection to cricket came through the radio, with all its static, score updates and voices of the commentators breaking in with sudden excitement. And now, in front of me, was the real thing. I didn't know all the players, but they were cricketers. Real ones. I remember inching closer to the dressing room area, notebook in hand, heart pounding, unsure if I was even allowed there. Dressing rooms weren't gated like they are now. There was a kind of gentle porousness to it all. I remember nervously walking up, hoping someone would sign my notebook. And someone did. I don't remember who. I wasn't even brave enough to ask, but I remember staring at that autograph the whole way home.

That was the day Karnataka scored 196, with PV Shashikanth carrying his bat for 103 not out and Anil Kumble taking four wickets, though I didn't know it at the time. I wasn't there to understand the strategy or the scoreboard. I was there because of a feeling. That quiet rush of being part of something bigger, even for an afternoon.

And now, three decades since my first-ever live match in a stadium and the three recent Test matches that brought back the child in me, here I was. Sitting in a Surry Hills pub in Sydney with two Sainik School alumni, having just finished watching a memorable match and series. A reunion that wasn't planned or ceremonial, just casual, comfortable and unexpectedly meaningful.

There was something poetic about the whole thing; I can vividly remember the feeling as I walked back to Central Station to catch the light rail. I walked away that night with a kind of quiet fullness. The match had ended, the Test was done, but the game – the real one, the one that lives off the field – was still very much on.

CHAPTER 5

THE GAME CONTINUES

Hey, friend. If you've made it this far – thank you.

The past three chapters were a recollection (and occasional commentary) on one unforgettable summer I spent chasing cricket across three cities. From the echoing tunnels of the Gabba to panoramic seats of the MCG and the pink haze of the SCG, I've tried to capture what it feels like to be inside the game as a fan, not a player. But if you thought the story ended with the final ball in Sydney, you'd be mistaken.

Because anything you follow passionately tends to follow you back.

And cricket? Cricket came with me. What follows in these pages contains no match recaps, no crowd chants, no player stats. You won't find a single delivery bowled. But cricket will still be there, quietly embedded in every moment that unfolded after I stepped out of the stadium. It was in the people I met, the old connections rekindled, the new ones sparked, and the unexpected moments of generosity, mentorship and meaning.

This is a chapter about how sport leaves the ground and enters your life. About how cricket, in particular, has a way of stitching itself into your world not just as a game, but as a thread that weaves people, places and purpose together.

So, let's continue. The match might be over. But the story isn't.

...

Someone once said the best time to reflect is when your suitcase won't shut.

Okay, no one said that, but I was feeling it. The sting of India's loss in Sydney was still fresh, but oddly, I found myself feeling grateful for it. If the match had gone all five days, I don't know how I'd have managed to pack. The extra two days gave me something I hadn't had in weeks: time. Time to sift through receipts, pull shirts off hangers and reckon with the sheer volume of stuff I'd purchased over three matches and three cities.

I had bought more memorabilia than meals. T-shirts from the MCG. Programs. Multiple cricket balls stamped with the MCG logo. Five signed copies of Pat Cummins's book, all still wrapped in the bookstore's gold-edged ribbon. I removed two shirts, rolled up three pairs of jeans and finally gave in. I bought an extra suitcase. It ended up becoming my cricket bag, but not the kind with pads and gloves. This one was full of memories.

But I didn't buy any of this for myself.

Most of the souvenirs were meant for others. People who had, in some shape or form, been part of this journey. Some were old friends, some new acquaintances, and a few were Twitter handles who had become steady presences in my inbox. These were the people who replied to my match updates, kept up with my weather forecasts, and stayed awake at 4.30 am India time just to send me emoji reactions. I may have been physically alone in the stadiums, but I never felt lonely. Every pull shot, every wicket, every moment of tension, I was sharing with them, one message at a time.

And I wanted to give them something in return.

Not generic duty-free chocolates or souvenir koalas but gifts that carried the feeling of the summer I'd just lived through. A Boxing Day Test cap for my cousin's husband who'd followed every session. A cricket ball for a young player in Bangalore. (I still can't come around to calling it Bengaluru.) The signed Pat Cummins book for people I knew would truly treasure it. These weren't flashy gestures. They were acknowledgements. Tokens of shared passion. Proof they were part of this with me, even if their names were never on a ticket.

I've always believed that if you're going to give someone a gift, it should be something they'd never think to buy for themselves, but will never want to part with once they have it. That's what I was aiming for. Souvenirs that weren't just souvenirs. They were keepsakes. From a summer that had already become a memory, given back to the people who made it feel like something more.

By the morning of 8 January, everything had somehow fit. I'd wrangled the zippers, weighed the bags twice and sacrificed a few more T-shirts, but it all fit. So, with my cricket-stamped souvenirs safely packed into their own dedicated suitcase, I headed for the airport.

The plan was to land in Bangalore and then take a short domestic flight to Hubli, aka Hubballi, the nearest airport to my hometown Dharwad. I'd spend a few quiet days there with my family before returning to Bangalore for my cousin's wedding. For the first time in nearly eight years, I was going to spend more than just a few fleeting hours in Bangalore. I'd blocked out a solid stretch – nearly four weeks – in India and I hoped for at least a solid week in Bangalore, the city that had once been mine.

...

At Sydney Airport, I was at the JB Hi-Fi billing counter (an electronics store, for those not familiar), clutching a power bank and waiting for the cashier when I saw him. KL Rahul. Just a few feet in front of me. Athiya Shetty, his wife and a Bollywood actor, stood beside him, silent, sunglasses still on indoors. He was dressed simply, hoodie half-zipped, face unmistakably tired, not in the jet-lagged, had-a-long-day kind of way, but in the way only a month-long Test series can leave you.

The fan in me twitched. He was right there. All I had to do was get closer and say hello, maybe sneak in a photo. But I didn't move. I didn't even reach for my phone. Instead, I stood still, choosing to be an observer in that buzzing corridor of fluorescent lights and yellow price charts.

Because at that moment, he wasn't a cricketer. He was just a man, finally off the field, trying to melt into the background with his wife by his side. He looked like someone who deserved rest, not recognition. And, for the first time in my life, I didn't see him as someone I wanted a selfie with. I saw him as someone I understood. So I let it be. No selfies, no fanfare. Just a silent nod as our eyes met and the both of us went on with our lives.

Funny how that works. Years ago, I ran into Morne Morkel and Daniel Sims at the airport and couldn't contain my excitement. Got my daughter to say hi and even snapped some pictures. Back then, the thrill was in the moment. Now, it was in the restraint. Maybe that's what time and a summer like this one does to you; it changes what you chase.

A few hours later, I boarded my flight to Bangalore and promptly knocked out for most of the twelve-hour haul. No in-flight movies, no half-hearted attempts at reading, just sleep.

In Bangalore, I had just enough of a layover to walk through the newly renovated terminal. Sleek. Polished. Almost unrecognisable from the one I remembered. For a moment, it felt like I'd landed in Singapore, not South India.

Soon enough, I was on the short flight northward to Hubli, the closest airport to my hometown of Dharwad. A quiet few days awaited me there, and I welcomed them with open arms. My wife and daughters had arrived from Pune just days earlier, staying with my parents while I crisscrossed cricket grounds on the other side of the country. When I stepped through the gates of home, the noise of the series finally dropped away. No crowds, no commentary, no scoreboard ticking in the background. Just my kids, tugging at my sleeves, asking if we could go to the farm.

We did, of course. My mother runs a mango orchard in Dharwad with about a hundred trees, all planted over the years with quiet ambition and stubborn care. She calls it Krishna Vana (Krishna's Garden), named after the god she's always kept close. We spent slow mornings there. The girls running between the trees, barefoot and shrieking, while I sat with a steel tumbler of coffee, just ... sitting. No phone, no meetings, no match updates. I couldn't remember the last time I'd had so much time without needing to be anywhere. At night, we lit a campfire in the open patch behind the house. The stars came out, and the kids kept trying to toast imaginary marshmallows on sticks we found in the shed.

In between the calm, work still threaded itself through my days. My wife and I were both working Australia hours, which sounds manageable until you throw in two young kids. So we rented cubicles in one of Dharwad's many 24/7 student libraries – a perk of being in a city known for its academics. They were usually filled with competitive exam aspirants, each one bent over notebooks and textbooks, chasing something bigger. It wasn't your usual workplace; ambition hung in the air like incense. For many, this was more than just an exam. It was a lifeline. A way to lift themselves beyond what their parents could afford, or even imagine. Some had come from other states, drawn by Dharwad's reputation as an academic hub. Sitting there with my headphones on, answering emails, it was hard not to feel moved by the quiet determination around me. These weren't study tables. They were launchpads.

Apart from family and work, there wasn't much else on the agenda, and that was the point. I took the girls out for drives, ate homemade food and watched the light flicker across my childhood bedroom. Some days, my parents would take the kids to the farm, and I'd use the quiet to catch up on work or walk the streets I once cycled down as a teenager. On one weekend, we drove out to Dandeli – a short family trip, nothing too elaborate but a good reminder of how different a river looks when no one's trying to compare it to a fast bowler.

These weren't days I'll remember for what happened. I'll remember them for what didn't. No screens, no commentary and no new cities every week – just a long exhale after a summer that had filled me to the brim. Yet, even in that stillness, cricket was never far. I could feel it in the weight of the souvenirs I'd brought, now carefully tucked away in a corner of my suitcase. Waiting for their moment.

...

A couple of days in we celebrated *Sankranti* at my mum's farm. It was a simple evening with neighbours and family, some traditional sweets and a quick photo session in the mango orchard. In that celebration, though, all my plans changed.

You know how in every town there's that one person who somehow knows everyone? That's my uncle, Dr Shankar Bijapur. My mother's younger brother and constant guide and inspiration throughout my life. He's a highly accomplished IVF specialist, with an MBA from one of India's top MBA colleges and an entrepreneur with experience building and running large-scale medical facilities. Unofficially though, he's the local connector-in-chief actively involved in many social and professional organisations. Toastmasters? Check. Mentor young entrepreneurs? Check. He's quite the institution in this part of the world. Mention a name and chances are he not only knows them, but also helped them start their family. (Quite literally!) He'll never brag, but you'll hear a gentle, 'Ah, yes, I know them,' followed by a story involving a clinic visit, a family milestone, or maybe even where they get their dosa from. He's the kind of person whose, 'I'll handle it,' is less a promise and more a certain declaration.

So, when I casually mentioned I'd love to meet a few entrepreneurs while I was in town, he simply nodded and said, 'I'll connect you with someone.'

Sure enough, not even an hour later, my phone rang. 'Nikya, how are you, man?'

Only a handful of people in the world call me that anymore.

Turns out the person on the other end of the line was Rohan Kulkarni, my actual bench mate from school. Someone I hadn't seen or spoken to in quite a few years. He'd somehow gone from classroom pranks to running the local TiE chapter (The Indus Entrepreneurs, a global network that supports entrepreneurship). And, without skipping a beat he said, 'We've got a major event coming up. Karnataka's IT minister is the chief guest. We'd love for you to give the keynote.'

I immediately said yes, but the situation was more complicated than that because now, any hope of spending extended time in Bangalore while catching up with friends, revisiting favourite restaurants, and leisurely distributing the souvenirs I brought disappeared. I'd been hoping to hand them out slowly while sitting with friends, chatting about the matches, when I'd pull out a hat or a book and say, 'This reminded me of you.'

Instead, I had to rethink everything. I found myself mentally scrolling through names. Was anyone still in Hubli or Dharwad? Anyone I could possibly catch at the wedding? The answers, unfortunately, were no and no. Everyone I was hoping to meet was in Bangalore, which meant they'd have to wait for their presents and I wouldn't have enough time to hand them all out in person.

The week that followed was a blur. Between keynote prep (it went really well!), suit shopping for my cousin's wedding (there was a dress code to be followed), and last-minute packing (again!), I found myself ricocheting across Hubli like a courier with a cricket problem. I managed to squeeze in a Savaji meal (definitely check it out if you're in North Karnataka some time), a few half-finished workdays and some early morning walks through familiar lanes that hadn't changed nearly as much as I had. But before I could catch my breath, it was time to head to Bangalore.

It was 3 February, my cousin Chinmay's wedding day. Now, Chinmay is a hardcore Royal Challengers Bangalore (RCB) men's team and Virat Kohli fan, and we've shared many highs and lows of RCB's campaigns over the years. The running joke in the family, which is indeed a fact, is that RCB have lost whenever I've watched their matches, especially the crucial ones. So, as a wedding gift for Chinmay, I decided not to watch any of RCB's matches in the 2025 season. And what happened? RCB men's team became the IPL champions after eighteen long years. As an RCB tragic, I couldn't be happier myself. The things you have to do for your favourite franchise and your close family! Sometimes, the best you can do as a cricket fan is to not watch cricket. Perfectly reasonable, no?

Spread over nearly two days, the wedding itself was a lot of fun. What made it special was that it was the first Indian wedding our kids were attending and it'd be the first ever wedding memory for our elder one. There's something to be said about the food at Indian weddings and I didn't miss any chance to dive into the multi-cuisine delicacies served up over those two days. My daughters had a great time dressing up in traditional clothes, joining the *baaraat* (the wedding procession), and even putting together an impromptu dance show on the reception night. It was such a heartfelt family get together and we were so glad the timing had all worked out for us to attend the wedding.

Chinmay (the groom) and Janhavi (his sister) are my immediate cousins, my aunt Uma's children, and all of us have shared so many special memories over the years, many around cricket too. And it was only apt that we were all coming together again for another special memory, and with cricket as the backdrop.

On the following day, as the last of the rituals wound down, my mind was already somewhere else – on a promise I'd made, and a person I was finally about to meet. That evening, as the celebrations gave way to goodbyes, we stepped out of the wedding and into a cab. I was going to see someone I'd only ever known through WhatsApp messages and the sound of bat meeting ball.

...

I was standing inside the gates of the New Innings Cricket Enterprise, better known as NICE Academy. It was a late afternoon in Bangalore, right during that brief window where the sun hasn't fully given up but the heat has. I could hear the snap of leather on turf, the soft shuffle of footsteps at the crease, and the odd grunt from the nets. It was quiet, but not still. Focused, like the place had its own rhythm.

And there, walking toward me in a sun-faded cap and sneakers that looked like they'd outlasted a few seasons, was Arjun Dev, NICE's head coach. We'd been exchanging messages for the better part of a year with videos, updates and the occasional cricket rant, but this was our first proper meeting.

A quick intro about Arjun: he doesn't fit the stereotypical image of a cricket coach. There's no booming voice, no chest-thumping pep talks, no clipboard choreography. What you notice first about him is a quiet clarity that suggests he knows exactly what he's building.

He runs the NICE Academy less like a coaching centre and more like a fiercely focused training ground. It's not the flashiest set-up, but that's not what Arjun's after. His eye is always on the long game. Over the years, he's earned a reputation for spotting talent early, and more importantly, knowing how to nurture it. One of his students, Shreyanka Patil, now plays for the Indian women's team and the Royal Challengers Bangalore. But, if you ask Arjun, he'll tell you she's only just getting started, and so is he.

What sets him apart isn't just the players he's helped shape but the philosophy that guides him. He's not interested in manufacturing athletes. He's invested in building people, especially girls from smaller towns and underrepresented backgrounds, who often don't get the facilities, exposure or belief that the game demands. For Arjun, coaching isn't a job. It's a kind of crusade, and it shows when you talk to him. He trains them, supports them, advocates for them, and sometimes even finds ways to keep them in the game when the world around them isn't ready to support that.

Okay, time for a backstory. Arjun and I, we didn't meet through some big cricketing event or shared circle. Our connection started, as these things in my life often do, with a message. Back in March 2024, I'd reached out to congratulate him on Shreyanka Patil's stand-out season with RCB and their win in the Women's Premier League. I'd followed her journey for years and knew Arjun had coached her from the ground up. That message turned into a conversation about talent, about opportunity, and about girls' cricket in India. Somewhere in that exchange, I told him I was keen to support upcoming players, especially from North Karnataka. 'Even if it's just one bat,' I said, 'let me know.' And he did.

Arjun told me about a girl named Inchara. He shared a video of her batting, and you could tell she was trying to make every shot count. She had this spark that he described as the kind that doesn't show up every day. I asked him what she needed most, and like most cricketers, the answer was simple: a good bat. So, he went to a local shop, scanned a QR code, and I sent over the money. That bat became the first thin thread in what's since become a long, winding tapestry.

From there, we kept in touch. Arjun would send occasional updates – short clips from the nets, a quick note about how Inchara was progressing, or a match summary he thought I'd enjoy. With a million other things on his plate, it was generous of him to still keep me in the loop. He knew I cared. And I did. Watching someone grow from behind the scenes like that ... it pulls you in.

Over time, the updates became more frequent. There were milestones: a fifty in a boys' game, a gritty knock on a tough pitch, even an injury scare that thankfully turned out to be just a tactical retirement. I started to feel like I was part of her journey in some tiny, long-distance way.

I wasn't doing much. A bat here, some gear there. But the way Arjun spoke about these girls, it was impossible not to root for them. Not only because they were talented, but because they were trying to make something happen in places where the world didn't always look.

And in a quiet way, all of this had started to matter more to me than I'd expected. It wasn't a grand plan. I didn't sit down one day and say, 'Let's go support young women cricketers.' It just unfolded. One message, one bat, one story at a time.

Back to the present.

It felt unreal seeing Inchara in person. After a year of WhatsApp updates, short clips, scorecards, and the occasional 'Look at this drive' messages, I'd built a version of her in my head. And there she was, younger than I'd imagined, but also way more driven than most kids her age. There was no flashiness, no big swagger. Just a calm sort of focus, like she already knew what she was chasing.

Arjun also introduced me to Shreya. Feisty wicketkeeper, he said. Studying hard, playing harder. We talked for a bit before he mentioned that she was from Bijapur, where I went to school, and it brought back memories.

I'd been lugging souvenirs across multiple cities and family events – bucket hats from the Gabba, Boxing Day shirts, Pink Test caps, and a few other odds and ends I'd picked up along the way. This was the moment I'd been waiting for since I packed them. It wasn't about the stuff itself, just the idea of passing on something from that wild Summer of Cricket to the girls actually out there chasing it.

And then something really lovely happened. I didn't plan it, and I'm glad I didn't because it wouldn't have felt the same. My daughter and the two girls just started chatting, and before long, they were playing cricket in the nets. Inchara and Shreya took turns bowling to my daughter. Just the three of them, figuring it out together. I stood off to the side, taking it in. It was one of those moments you don't need to photograph because you know it's going to stay with you anyway. (Though I did later, because who wouldn't want to capture that moment for their daughter's memory?)

Watching the three of them, one just starting to discover the game, the other two already deep into the grind of it, felt oddly full circle. I didn't say much, just stood there, hoping that my daughter would remember this. Not the stats, not the souvenirs, but this moment: of being welcomed into a game she's learning to love, by someone who's fighting every day to stay in it. It made me think about what cricket had meant to me growing up, the way it shaped my routines, my friendships, my imagination. And how, now, it was slowly starting to shape hers too. If even a sliver of that stuck with her, I'd be more than content. And maybe that's part of why all this matters so much to me. I do want my daughter to have as many role models as she can. Not just the household names like Ellyse Perry – who, by the way, is her current favourite – but girls she can actually see, meet, maybe even hit a few balls with. Someone whose journey doesn't feel a world away.

As the girls took turns, Arjun and I found ourselves leaning against the nets, watching them and chatting. It was one of those easy conversations where the cricket kept running in the background but the real subject was something deeper. That's when I brought up something I'd been thinking about for a while: the Daughters and Dads program.

I told him how, just a few weeks before this trip, I'd signed up for the program in Sydney. It was a nine-week initiative run by Cricket Australia and all the state associations, designed to help fathers and daughters bond over sport. Each session was about ninety minutes long and included a mix of warm-ups, batting and bowling drills, catching practice and short games. The daughters led most of the activity while the dads played a supporting role. The focus was on fun and participation between the daughters and their parents. No coaching, no pressure, just showing up, being present, and doing it together.

The magic of it wasn't in the batting or the warm-ups, it was in the bond. In dads learning how to listen, and girls learning how to speak up. It was in moments like when my daughter corrected my grip or called me out for crowding her stance. It was in the sideways glances, the high-fives, the goofy cheers. It was in watching a roomful of men, many of them awkward at first, grow into better teammates, not just for their daughters, but for the idea of girls in sport.

Then I pitched an idea to him, of having something similar in India. Arjun listened carefully, nodded, and we kicked off a longer conversation. I'm keen for that to happen. (And hey, if you're reading this and think you can help make it real, let me know!)

...

We said our goodbyes as the nets began to empty out, with the late evening sun giving the turf a last golden rinse. I tucked the leftover souvenirs back into my bag, shook Arjun's hand, and promised to keep him posted. The cab ride back from NICE Academy was quiet, partly because my daughter fell asleep almost instantly, but mostly because my mind was still replaying the whole day. It had been a lot. A lot of emotion, a lot of meaning. But also, a quiet kind of fulfillment.

Back home, I fully opened the big suitcase I'd been lugging across cities and countries – although a little lighter now after handing out some souvenirs at Arjun's academy. One by one, I laid them out on the bed and the whole trip came back to me as a highlight reel. These were for people who'd made this series feel bigger than the matches alone. People who weren't in the stands, but who were somehow right there with me. Now it was time to play postman. So, the next morning, the deliveries began.

First up was Monil, my cousin Janhavi's husband who was a constant WhatsApp companion throughout the summer. I properly caught up with him at a post-wedding ritual. He was busy during the actual wedding playing multiple roles – in cricketing parlance, he switched between team manager to the twelfth man ferrying drinks. When we did indeed get some quiet time together, it was not a long-drawn discussion, just some heartfelt smiles and quips that kindred souls share. He's one of those fans who treats Test cricket like a religion, complete with 4.30 am alarms and tactical WhatsApp commentary during tea breaks. I was the on-the-ground weather correspondent, he was the armchair analyst from India. I gave him the Boxing Day Test sweatshirt, hat and some Pink Test memorabilia. He'd been there with me in spirit, every over.

My cousin Chinmay, the groom, and his wife got slightly different gifts compared to what I'm guessing they got for the wedding – MCG hoodies. The best wedding gift for a cricket follower if you ask me!

Then came the five copies of Pat Cummins's book, *Tested*. There was something oddly satisfying about passing them on to people who'd followed the series as closely as I had. I liked the idea of those books landing on desks and shelves in cities across India, each carrying a little echo of the summer we'd lived through, even if we weren't sitting in the same stands.

One had gone to Arjun, obviously. Another to Ritesh Banglani when we finally met in person over coffee a few days later. The meeting almost didn't happen because I forgot the gift bag at home and had to turn around, but Ritesh, ever gracious, waited. He's someone who's been deep in the ecosystem far longer than I have, and between the two of us, we've seen India's startup world stretch and mutate over the past two decades. Yet somehow, we'd never met. We shared countless connections, mutual friends, threads on Twitter, even startup war stories. And yet, it was cricket, not startup ideas or venture capital funding, that finally got us to sit down together.

It was funny, actually. In a Bangalore cafe usually reserved for funding conversations and pitch decks, our table was cluttered with Test match souvenirs and stories about stadiums, cover drives and our own cricket obsessions. I imagine anyone eavesdropping would've been thoroughly confused. Sure, we touched on startups – it's hard not to when you're with a venture capitalist like Ritesh – but the centre of gravity that day was unmistakably cricket. And through it all, what stood out was how generous he was with his time, especially on short notice. It didn't feel like a first meeting. It felt like cricket had sneakily staged a reunion we never knew we needed.

One more went to Sanjay Swamy. If you've spent any time in India's startup world, you already know the name. One of the key minds behind Aadhaar, Sanjay's the sort of person who blends deep tech with deep cricket, a rare and brilliant combo. We've known each other for years and followed each other's musings on Twitter, but hadn't met in a long time. I'd hoped to catch him this time, but we couldn't make it work. So, I sent a package instead. In that bag, alongside a book and some memorabilia, was also a nod to a long, oddly intersecting connection.

As well as that package, I sent another for Amit, his colleague at Prime Venture Partners, someone I remembered was also a huge cricket fan. We hadn't spoken in a while, but the thought of him seeing a bag full of Test memorabilia made me smile.

And the delivery? All thanks to Swiggy. A few taps on my phone and the parcels zipped across the city while I stayed put. If I'd tried doing it myself, say from Indiranagar to Whitefield, I'd probably still be waiting for the signal to turn green. So yes, this book also contains some unsolicited, unpaid gratitude to India's real MVPs: the ones who deliver. (Not sponsored. But if Swiggy wants to talk, you know where to find me.)

A few days later, I got a message saying they'd become the envy of the floor. Apparently, the memorabilia had done a few rounds before finally landing on their desks.

I know how all this might sound, me handing out signed books and limited-edition memorabilia like some travelling cricket Santa. But honestly, that's not what this was. The thing is, I didn't choose these people because they were famous or influential. I chose them because, over the last few months, they'd felt like fellow passengers. Some I'd known for years. Some I barely knew. But we spoke the same language – the language of scorecards and cover drives, of fourth-innings tension and rain-ruined draws, of staying up way too late for a Test match that probably wouldn't end well. We'd all felt the same beats, hope, heartbreak and quiet awe of being part of something bigger than ourselves. So, lugging half a suitcase of cricket gear across cities didn't feel like a chore. It felt like closure.

And, in some odd way, giving those gifts felt like the final over of the tour. An epilogue and one last offering before I packed it all away and got on a flight back to Sydney. Back to life.

I said I bought five books and I handed out four in Bangalore. So, what about the fifth? It sits proudly on my bookshelf, a constant and happy reminder of an incredible summer and all the fantastic experiences and people that came with it. And it's now all wrapped together in this very book, which will proudly sit next to Pat Cummins's in my bookshelf – and hopefully in the cricket section of bookstores all over.

POSTSCRIPT

The final words of this book were written on 4 August 2025, the very day India clinched arguably one of its most dramatic Test match victories ever, defeating England by a mere six runs at The Oval to level the series 2–2. The whole series, this specific test match, and the fifth day's play in particular, were a perfect advertisement for Test cricket.

The images of Chris Woakes walking out to bat with a dislocated shoulder and Mohammed Siraj fittingly getting the last wicket will be forever etched in every cricket lover's minds. Who says Test cricket is slow-paced? I couldn't even catch a breath for the whole of this series!

Cricket is a game of glorious uncertainties. But no one really tells you how quickly the ground can shift under your feet. It's been about six months since India's tour to Australia ended, and yet the landscape already feels unrecognisable.

Virat Kohli and Rohit Sharma, both gone from the longest format. The giants who once carried Indian Test cricket are now watching from the sidelines, Shubman Gill has taken over as captain of the Test team and is suddenly the face of Indian cricket's next era.

On the other side of the scoreboard, Sam Konstas, the breakout star of the Boxing Day Test and someone I wrote about with so much awe just a few chapters ago, hasn't found his rhythm since. The Australian media now call him a flop and say he has nowhere to hide. At the time, it felt like he had that X-factor – the edge, the intent, the uncut diamond potential. But maybe a bit more polish was needed. Or maybe the stars just aren't aligning right now. Either way, the contrast is striking.

Australia, too, lost the World Test Championship final to South Africa. From the highs of the Border–Gavaskar Trophy to the lows of a title slip, they've been tested, though they've had solid wins in Sri Lanka and the West Indies.

England, for their part, are going through their ebbs and flows. With their Bazball approach, they've been blowing hot and cold – chasing over 350 in one match then losing by nearly the same margin in another. The buzz around Bazball doesn't feel quite as loud anymore.

So yes, things change. Fast. But cricket remains as unpredictable and addictive as ever. There's no shortage of storylines. In just a few months, England will be back in Australia for the Ashes. India will tour again too; this time for white-ball cricket. And who knows what those matches will bring?

Off the cricket field, Bharat Sundaresan is now part of the 2025 AIYD delegation, via an introduction I made to Aman Gaur. My own little contribution to bringing Australia and India even closer! Crazy how it all comes together. Bharat also had a happy reunion recently with Patrick Patterson in the Caribbean, eight years after his masterpiece that bowled us over.

As I type this, I can't help but wonder: if all this happened in just six months, what might the next summer hold? Maybe nothing. Maybe everything. Maybe even another book.

Let's see.

"Stop the press!"

Oh, and I managed to squeeze this in just moments before the book went to print. Cheteshwar Pujara has announced his retirement from international cricket. May this book be a tribute to his stellar service to the game. Quite a full circle that I started the book reminiscing about my passionate following for him and now wrapping it up with his retirement news.

ACKNOWLEDGEMENTS

Writing is always a personal endeavour – writing an entire book even more so. Yet bringing a book into the world is a collective effort, and this one would not have been possible without the belief, support and blessings of so many people.

First and foremost, my heartfelt thanks to my publisher, Jessica Mudditt, and the wonderful team at Hembury Books – editors Deborah Shaw and Meg English, designer Zalia Lackey, editorial coordinator Sinead Heap, and publishing coordinator Earl Pamplona. Your guidance and care have shaped this book, and I would warmly recommend working with Jessica and Hembury Books to anyone considering publishing a book. Thanks to Drew Ambrose for referring Hembury Books to me.

Huge thanks to Sathwik Billa for the creativity, ideas, and energy he brought from the earliest days – his support enriched the journey of bringing my story to life. I'd also like to thank Sparsh Chattani for her support across my various initiatives, including the book's promotion.

It takes early believers to give an idea its wings. I am deeply grateful to Bharat Sundaresan, Sidin Vadukut, Simon Taufel and Lisa Sthalekar for their generous endorsements. Seeing words of encouragement from such accomplished voices in cricket and literature on the pages of my book is a true highlight of my life. I am also thankful to Molina Asthana and Geoff Verco for their belief in both me and the book, as well as for the introductions they facilitated. My gratitude to Arjun Dev for his whole-hearted support and for giving me the opportunity to play a small part in nurturing upcoming talent in India. A special thanks to Nonnie Noffke for her support of the book and Ashley Noffke for the kind words, and to Professor Philip Morgan for his warm engagement and encouragement. Many thanks to Gitesh Agarwal for his endorsement.

To the many people who feature in these pages through the conversations and moments we shared during that unforgettable summer – thank you. I will cherish those memories for a long time. It's no surprise they inspired me to write a whole book!

The Australia-India bilateral connection runs as a constant thread through this book and through my own journey. I am grateful to those leading this space for their vision and encouragement – Warren Kirby MP, Irfan Malik, Poornima Menon, Sonia Sadiq Gandhi, the Australia India Youth Dialogue (AIYD), the Australia India Business Council (AIBC) and the Centre for Australia India Relations (CAIR).

My close family has been a constant source of love and encouragement. Though we haven't been able to spend much time together since my move to Australia, they will always remain special. I'm grateful to my uncle Dr. Shankar for all his guidance and mentorship and to my aunt Uma for all the love and care over the years. I'm sending lots of love to my cousins – Janhavi and her husband Monil, Chinmay and his wife Vinati, and Pranav and Atharv. To my sister Neha, thank you for all the wonderful memories we've created together. And to my in-laws Usha and Vishwanath, thank you for your constant encouragement and heartfelt blessings.

To my parents Indira and Narasinharao, who have been an incredible source of strength and support. My passion for pursuing my interests comes from my mother, whose own dedication to her interests continues to inspire me every day.

To my daughters – Neeti, my wise conscience keeper who reminds me of what truly matters (and even offered her own critique for this book), and Keerti, my glorious bundle of energy and joy. I am deeply grateful to be their dad and hope this book makes them proud.

Finally, to my source of light and strength – my wife Deepti. This book, like so much in my life, would not have been possible without your unwavering support. Nurturing a young family while balancing our ambitious careers and community commitments is no small feat, and I am profoundly grateful for the time, space and encouragement you give me to follow my passions. It means the world to me.

www.ingramcontent.com/pod-product-compliance
Lightning Source LLC
Chambersburg PA
CBHW020414080526
44584CB00014B/1319